INTEGRATING INSPECTION MANAGEMENT INTO YOUR QUALITY IMPROVEMENT SYSTEM

Also Available from ASQ Quality Press:

The Management System Auditor's Handbook
Joe Kausek

Process Quality Control: Troubleshooting and Interpretation of Data, Fourth Edition
Ellis R. Ott, Edward G. Schilling, and Dean V. Neubauer

Decision Process Quality Management
William D. Mawby

The Handbook of Applied Acceptance Sampling: Plans, Procedures and Principles
Kenneth S. Stephens

Unlocking the Power of Your QMS: Keys to Business Performance Improvement
John E. (Jack) West and Charles A. Cianfrani

Product Liability Prevention: A Strategic Guide
Randall L. Goodden

Design for Six Sigma as Strategic Experimentation: Planning, Designing, and Building World-Class Products and Services
H.E. Cook

Value-Driven Channel Strategy: Extending the Lean Approach
R. Eric Reidenbach and Reginald W. Goeke

To request a complimentary catalog of ASQ Quality Press publications, call 800-248-1946, or visit our website at http://qualitypress.asq.org.

INTEGRATING INSPECTION MANAGEMENT INTO YOUR QUALITY IMPROVEMENT SYSTEM

William D. Mawby

ASQ Quality Press
Milwaukee, Wisconsin

American Society for Quality, Quality Press, Milwaukee 53203
© 2006 ASQ
All rights reserved. Published 2005
Printed in the United States of America

12 11 10 09 08 07 06 05   5 4 3 2 1

Library of Congress Cataloging-in-Publication Data

Mawby, William D., 1952-
  Integrating inspection management into your quality improvement system /
William D. Mawby.
    p. cm.
  Includes bibliographical references and index.
  ISBN-13: 978-0-87389-665-8 (softcover)
  ISBN-10: 0-87389-665-3 (softcover)
  1. Quality control. 2. Production management. I. Title.

  TS156.M3875 2005
  658.5'68--dc22
                                    2005019124

ISBN-13: 978-0-87389-665-8
ISBN-10: 0-87389-665-3

Publisher: William A. Tony
Acquisitions Editor: Annemieke Hytinen
Project Editor: Paul O'Mara
Production Administrator: Randall Benson

ASQ Mission: The American Society for Quality advances individual,
organizational, and community excellence worldwide through learning,
quality improvement, and knowledge exchange.

Attention Bookstores, Wholesalers, Schools, and Corporations: ASQ Quality Press
books, videotapes, audiotapes, and software are available at quantity discounts
with bulk purchases for business, educational, or instructional use.
For information, please contact ASQ Quality Press at 800-248-1946, or write to
ASQ Quality Press, P.O. Box 3005, Milwaukee, WI 53201-3005.

To place orders or to request a free copy of the ASQ Quality Press Publications
Catalog, including ASQ membership information, call 800-248-1946. Visit our
Web site at www.asq.org or http://qualitypress.asq.org.

 Printed on acid-free paper

Quality Press
600 N. Plankinton Avenue
Milwaukee, Wisconsin 53203
Call toll free 800-248-1946
Fax 414-272-1734
www.asq.org
http://qualitypress.asq.org
http://standardsgroup.asq.org
E-mail: authors@asq.org

*With love and respect for my wife, LuAnne,
and my daughter, Briana, for their unfailing support
and encouragement of my efforts.*

Table of Contents

List of Figures and Tables

Preface

The inspection of product and process has been a mainstay of quality programs since the inception of manufacturing processes. Often this inspection was performed by the craftsman or creator of the product. The carpenter who had just shaped the table leg would also be the one to judge its fitness for use. The purpose of this inspection was to trigger and target corrective actions that would *improve the delivered quality*. This approach worked well as long as production was low and nothing needed to be standardized, but, as industry evolved, problems with this simple system became apparent. Gradually, the inspection function was segregated from the manufacturing function. Skilled inspectors were created whose chief function was not to manufacture, but rather to inspect and judge. Entire departments were created to maintain this inspection function and keep it independent of production demands. In the past and even today, this inspection function can account for a large part of a product's cost and require a significant part of a company workforce. Inspection has an extensive track record indicating that it can be an effective if sometimes expensive way in which to achieve higher quality product.

The quality revolution as practiced by Shewhart, Deming, Crosby, Juran, and others emphasized three aspects of quality:

1. Quality can have direct positive economic value.

2. The earlier the detection, the less costly the correction is.

3. Quality must be embedded into all facets of an organization.

There were many successes won through this approach, and these teachings are seen as fundamental truth by most modern quality managers. There have been many advancements of these methods and perhaps some repackaging into various programs such as statistical process control (SPC), total quality management (TQM), total productive maintenance (TPM), and continuous process improvement. The latest program that emphasizes these approaches and their statistical tools is Six Sigma. Six Sigma seems especially adept at creating an environment in which these methods can flourish and lead to gains when implemented through a project approach to continuous improvement. Most of these approaches focus on problem prevention as the most economic manner in which to improve outgoing quality.

So there is abundant evidence to support both inspection and continuous process improvement as valid approaches to improving delivered quality. Although it is often not stated, it seems clear that real quality programs should be constructed to blend the best features of each approach in the most advantageous way for a specific situation. For example, product inspection might be the more economical course when process improvements are not known or not feasible or not affordable. In other cases, it might be process inspection that is the best approach.

This book adopts the viewpoint that the best continuous improvement programs are a blend of product and process efforts. It is the effective integration of these efforts that determines the success of the quality effort, and that is the key to making rapid, economical advances in quality for the vast majority of manufacturing and services companies today and into the foreseeable future. Specifically, this book rests its approach on five observations:

1. Both products and processes must be continuously improved.

2. Inspections are the mode of implementing these improvements.

3. Inspection technology is improving radically.

4. Integration of inspection methods is powerful.

5. Quality can be strengthened and improved with integrated inspections.

The initial chapters of the book introduce sensors, measurements, and inspections. A classification of different inspection systems is introduced that is based on the type of action that is driven by the inspection. These three types of inspection process are: acceptance sampling methods, control methods, and adjustment methods. Each of these categories is populated with a rich tool set that is described in some detail. Demonstrations of how each tool can be optimized within a category are given. Later chapters explain how to integrate the individual tools into an effective system, both within a category and mixed among the three categories. That is, one may integrate a system of acceptance sampling plans purely or mixed acceptance sampling, control, and adjustment all in the same system. The penultimate chapter indicates how these integrated inspection systems can support Six Sigma and lean manufacturing efforts in aiding individual projects and in managing the overall program. The final chapter is an attempt to guess the future of continuous improvement as it might be impacted by enhancements in inspection process quality management.

The purpose of this book is to bring inspection-based systems into the light of modern quality programs and show how they can, with integration, provide support for making big quality gains with little quality investment. This information could be an advantage for any company, small or large, manufacturing or service, that wants to play in the high quality ballpark but cannot afford the heavy upfront expenditures that are often necessary in traditional approaches. It is especially important for those companies that want to establish programs that will work for the foreseeable future as well as in today's challenging business world.

1

A Reintroduction to Inspection Management
The Types and Costs of Inspection

THE MANUFACTURER'S CHALLENGE

Imagine that you are a global manufacturer of flexible reinforced hoses for automobiles. Your business had been steady and secure over the last 30 years, but recently it feels like you are in the epicenter of a Richter 5 earthquake. Everybody seems to be running as fast as they can just to keep up with all the changes. This madness seems to have especially affected the original equipment automobile supplier who is the dedicated customer for your products. It seems like this giant with the big appetite has become incredibly demanding over the last 10 years. First, there is a 15% increase in the number of hose types, which requires a variety of equipment retooling and changing of part numbering schemes. Second, your partner establishes a new program that commits you to take out 2% of your cost each year over the next five years. Third, your customer wants you to be able to guarantee a 98% dependable supply chain for delivery of parts to any of its automobile assembly sites around the world. Fourth, you have to face and pass an audit every quarter that keeps getting more and more intrusive into your internal quality management process. Talk about micromanagement! And while you are still reeling from all these challenges, there is talk about moving quickly on other fronts including: just-in-time delivery, monitoring your inventories as if they were just an extension of your customer's warehouse, and delivering directly to its assembly plants instead of to a central distribution center. Some of these challenges are summarized here:

1. Fewer nonconforming products are delivered to the customer.

2. More diversified products are required.

3. Continuous decreases in cost of manufacture are demanded.

4. Greater reliability in delivery times is necessary.

5. Embedding in the customer supply chain is the norm.

6. Increased audits and micromanagement occur.

You have been in this business for a long while now and are no stranger to these kinds of demands. You have tried a couple of times to implement a quality improvement program, and the three-letter acronyms like SPC, TQM, and DOE are still ringing in the ears of the workforce. There have been some points of success in the material preparation shop, but for whatever reason, this approach never really penetrated the intimate workings of your organization. The audits were passed, but there were few bottom-line results that were gained from all the hard work. Most of your process improvement resources have been targeted to automating all the systems that you can in order to enable efficiency gains. All this new equipment has brought with it tremendous amounts of new and better data, but little of it is being effectively used by a workforce that has been slow to adapt to it. Your workforce is aging, but you have spent a lot of money on training new employees and recertifying veterans.

Though not by lack of effort, you know that one of your company's weaker systems is its quality management effort. Your quality has always been just good enough to be acceptable, but that was before all these new demands and initiatives were placed on you. You know that the system is strained to the point of breaking, and that it is only the experience and expertise of your final inspection crews that have been maintaining the as-delivered quality at an acceptable level. This method of delivering quality is becoming cost prohibitive, with nonquality expenditures sitting at 18% of the your total manufacturing cost with a rising trend. Your profit margin is getting cut extremely thin!

You know that you need to do something quickly, but you also know that you cannot afford to do anything drastic. Quality might be free once you have the systems up and running, but it usually takes a lot of up-front effort to get to that stage. Ideally, you need a plan to milk the current setup for improvements and then finance further gains with the profits from this improved efficiency. The last thing you need is to spend a lot of money (that you don't have) to foot the bill for starting up a major Six Sigma (Harry 1982) or lean manufacturing program. It might be all right for General Electric to spend a billion dollars to get its programs going, but you barely have thousands to do it. You know that such programs are a good long-term objective and you suspect that without them your company could fail, but how do you get there? How can you create a quality management program that effectively focuses your meager resources in the right direction without threatening the very survival of the concern?

AN ANSWER TO MODERN MANUFACTURING'S CHALLENGE

This scenario is very common in today's manufacturing world. It is replicated across all sectors of the economy, all sizes of company, and all geographical locations. Modern manufacturing has to produce the highest quality products at the lowest cost and deliver them worldwide with near-perfect timing. It has to do this in the face of the ever-present pressure from competitors, disruptions in the technological landscape, and the inertia of aging infrastructures. It is no wonder that many ventures fail each year and that more and more companies see quality management as a prerequisite for success. Results prove that many quality programs fail and most do not live up to their promises (English 1999). Companies often conclude that, although the principles of continuous quality improvement are valid, the actual implementation of them is nearly impossible to achieve in organizations that are faced with so many overwhelming challenges.

There is a feasible answer to these questions and a solution to these dilemmas. An effective, implementable approach can be found in the proper integration of the two traditional elements of product and process inspection powered by a continuous improvement metaprocess. This answer is *inspection process quality management*. In the 1980s and 1990s, quality gurus like W. Edwards Deming (Deming 1986), Philip Crosby (Crosby 1984), and Joseph Juran (Juran 1999) were hard at work trying to gain entry into the boardrooms and control rooms of Western manufacturing concerns. But, as in many rebellions, the rebels often overemphasized the purity and power of their own approaches to process improvement compared to the approaches that were already in place in many organizations for product improvement. This was justifiable at the time because the U. S. quality progress was stagnant and what little effort there was appeared to be focused entirely on final product inspection. These gurus were trying their best to cause a paradigm shift and needed all the leverage that they could get. But, in reality, it is only through an alternation of effort between process and product improvement that the highest levels of quality are reached. And inspection processes are the fundamental components behind both activities. Figure 1.1 illustrates the efforts of the continuous improvement activity.

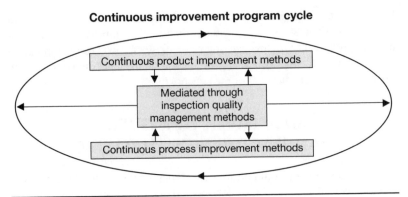

Figure 1.1 Continuous improvement of product and process through inspection.

The Nature of Inspections

Inspection (American Heritage Dictionary 1985) is the act of inspecting or the results of that inspection process. To *inspect* means to examine critically and carefully, especially for flaws. Notice that inspection brings with it a connotation of wisdom or intelligence. An inspection is the use of a measurement in an intelligent fashion to drive some corrective action. Inspections have long been associated with humans. It might be a visual inspection of a piece of fabric for coloration consistency. Or the inspection might be one of shape, size, or even weight. Inspections need not be restricted to product characteristics, however. It is also possible to look at a machine setup and determine if it is correct. Or one might compare the reading on the thermostat temperature gage with a subjective feeling of comfort. In an even wider sense, inspections can also be made of organization, functionality, and information.

The evaluation of inspections often involves human senses at some point, but this is not a strict requirement. Human senses can be supplemented by physical devices that are better at measuring temperature or pressure, for example. The human ability may also be enhanced with magnifying glasses or special lighting or an X-ray machine. Even the treatment of the data once they are received can be altered with special training or checklists or computerized expert systems. Finally, the correction process may be as simple as the turn of a control knob by the human operator, or it might be feedback to a material preparation area. It might be a warning to a later process stage to be aware that something odd might be coming down the line. It might also be an automatic control that is taken to correct the process for any upsets it has suffered.

Sometimes this evaluation process is handled through a very rapid interface, as in the flow meters in a chemical processing site where data can be updated in centiseconds. Other times this inspection can be a distinctly discrete set of actions that are widely separated in time, as would be the case of follow-up visits to a doctor after a medical treatment. Inspection processes are determined by various characteristics including the timing, duration, and intensity of the collections and the details of the postprocessing treatment. Poor choices of these control parameters can lead to poor inspection performance. Proper choices of these parameters can make it easier to integrate the various inspection systems into the overall production or service process. In this case one can hope to reap significant benefits. Inspection methods involve choices about:

1. The number of inspections

2. The placement of inspections

3. The types of inspections

4. The strength of inspections

5. The duration of inspections

6. The frequency of inspections

7. The timing of inspections

8. Filtering of inspections

9. Combining of inspections

10. Treatment of inspections

Measurements and Inspections

A *measurement* (American Heritage Dictionary 1985) is the result or act of ascertaining the dimensions, quantity, or capacity of something. A *measurement* is a way of converting an observed process, state, or condition into a quantitative value that is of potential usefulness to a person who is interested in the process. Measurements are mediated through senses or sensors that capture the underlying physical phenomenon and convert it to a standardized scale. Measurements can be simple, such as a single temperature sensor in a delivery tube at a hydrocarbon plant; they can be of intermediate complexity, such as that of an in-line weight scale in a rubber processing plant; or they can be quite complex, as when an auditor judges the reliability of the computer technical support function.

Inspections have at least three components: acquisition, analysis, and application. Each of the components can range from being simple to complex. Not all components have to be simple or complex. It is possible to mix components of various levels together to achieve the desired results. For example, the temperature of a conference room might be measured by a simple wall thermostat. This might be analyzed in a rather complex fashion by several people attending a meeting in the room in different ways given their clothing, their consumption of cold or hot beverages, and their natural comfort level. Finally, a decision to adjust the thermostat might require the leader of the meeting to balance the needs of a minority with other issues such as company policy on thermostat settings. When humans or computers are involved in a particular step, it tends to get more complicated. As the inspections become faster, the analysis more automatic, and the corrections more moderate, the system tends to become simpler. Poor measurements often guarantee poor inspections, but it is not true that good measurements guarantee good inspections. Some of the ways in which inspections are mediated by measurement processes are:

1. Human faculties alone

2. Skilled or expert human faculties

3. Machine faculties alone

4. Machine-aided human faculties

5. Human-validated machine faculties

6. Groups of human faculties

7. Groups of machine faculties

8. Groups of machine-aided human faculties

General Requirements for Good Inspections

Because inspections are so critical in the acquisition of the information that drives the basis for action on the process, it is important that inspections be taken seriously. First, they must be thorough. One must make a list of all the important characteristics that are to be measured and must make this list known to the inspectors or the facilitators of the inspection system. The definitions of the characteristics must be well-documented and well-distributed throughout the organization. It is a very common mistake to assume that everyone has an equal understanding of the details of definition of each element of inspection. It can be very hard work to do this consolidation step well, and it can often eat up plenty of resource hours in the early stages of establishing the inspection system. One must also work hard to ensure that these definitions are kept up-to-date with any modifications to the system.

Second, inspections must be consistent. That is, the application of the measurement must be coordinated between different inspectors, different instruments, and under different environmental conditions. Large differences between inspection methods can lead quickly to bad decisions about actions. Again, training and audits are crucial in this area to create and maintain consistency. Keep in mind that there are two types of consistency to be maintained. First, there is consistency through time for a given inspection process. Second, there is the amount of agreement between any given inspection process and a qualified process for the same measurement.

A third requirement for good inspections is that they be enabling. That is, they must actually measure something useful. More often than not, inspections are taken at easy-to-access places in the process rather than at true points of impact in a process. For example, an extrusion process may be checked only at the beginning and end of a bobbin of material due to prohibitive cost. In this case, one cannot explicitly know what is happening to the middle of the bobbin. Or an inspection may only be made in normal working hours rather than for the after-hours crew. This may be easier logistically, but it can also lead to large potential lapses of inspection just where one might need them most. Another common lapse is caused by processes that are widely separated geographically, especially if there are satellite offices or processes. It is critical to think hard about the process and to create an inspection system that portrays the real system that is of interest for quality improvement efforts.

From a practical organizational viewpoint, inspections should be done by qualified people using capable devices in stable, properly maintained environments. Often it is best to keep inspection personnel separate from production personnel to avoid conflict of interest. Remuneration and rewards for inspection personnel should emphasis problem finding, but also communication of these findings back to appropriate personnel. Without some mechanism for using the inspection results to improve quality, there is really no value added for doing even a great inspection job. It is also important to keep the inspection job fresh by changing stations and allowing time to recover from the sometimes exhausting job of inspection. When inspection systems are more automatic and less based on human faculties, it is important to have some independent way to assess that they are still operating correctly.

A Classification of Inspection Based on Derived Actions

Because measurements and inspections can be taken on any product or process, it is not the source of the inspection that is critical in understanding them. Rather, it is the actions that are taken as a result of the inspections that are probably best to distinguish between the major types of inspection. For example, it is entirely possible to change a process setting or parameter based on the measurement and inspection of a piece of manufactured product. A weighing of product sample from an extrusion process may be enough to force a corrective action of the temperature or vault pressure because the link between these process parameters and the product characteristic is well known. Since the action is one of process modification, it should be thought of in this way even though the initiating measurement is on a product. Alternately, a process measurement might lead to the scrapping of a particular set of product, as in the case of a baker who discovered that his oven temperature was set way too low for proper conditions. This type of action should be thought of as product improvement even though the raw inspection is of a process parameter. Both of these actions are direct and immediate in their impact on the quality.

Another category of actions can be less direct and immediate. For example, a sampling of product might not lead to direct modification of product or process, but rather to an increase in sampling frequency or intensity. A marketing analysis might measure the reaction of a consumer to a new dishwasher product. This inspection can then lead to a campaign to reinforce the weak response or a redesign of the container. This type of action is certainly not direct or immediate, but can have long-term benefit to improvement efforts and is clearly founded on inspections. Another viable action for an inspection process is to wait and do nothing. Clearly, the choice of action is a critical component of the inspection process quality management. The characterization of choices will play a key role in subsequent chapters. Some of the types of inspected guided actions are:

1. No action

2. Stopping the process

3. Removal of a single product

4. Removal of a group of products

5. Rework of the single product

6. Scrapping of the single product

7. Modification of the inspection process

8. Control actions

9. Adjustment actions

10. Project initiation

INTEGRATED SOLUTIONS

Like many of the newer innovations in quality management and improvement, the basic tools of inspection process quality management are well-known and well-documented (Berk 1993), and have been so for decades. The primary tools of interest in this book are acceptance sampling (Schilling 1982), control charts (Montgomery 2001), and automatic feedback loops (Box 1976). Other tools or approaches such as auto-quality systems (Garvin 1988), fail-safes (Shingo 1987), and automatic in-line inspection are embedded in these categories. Although some details of each of these methods will be necessary to give in this book, it is assumed that the reader can get more information on these techniques from separate sources. This book will emphasize the use of these tools in effective inspection systems. Great emphasis will be placed on methods to tune these tools and to integrate them under the inspection quality management umbrella. This integration can transform what some might consider old technology into a powerful new paradigm. The incredible increases in the number and types of inspections made possible through modern automation and computerization makes them the ideal way in which companies can speed up and beef up their quality programs without breaking their budgets. Through these approaches, it is possible to turn continuous improvement into reality for many who might otherwise come up short in their efforts.

A *sensor* (American Heritage Dictionary 1985) is a device that receives and responds to a signal or stimulus. Sensors now exist for just about every type of interaction that one could wish to measure. These sensors can be so small and so inexpensive that often they can be embedded into systems at hundreds of distinct points (Huang 2003). Sensors can be unobtrusive enough to be swallowed or sophisticated enough to have several simultaneous functions, each with its own programmable logic. These sensors can send and store data into databases where they can be analyzed with computer programs, or they can be somewhat intelligent in their own right. Agent technology (Fudenberg 1998) can transform a passive sensor into an active agent at exactly the right point of the process to take effective action, somewhat like the famous Maxwell's demon (Prigogine 1984) of physics fame. Maxwell's demon is an imaginary being who sorts molecules by type as they bounce between two connecting containers. It was intended as part of an impossible thought experiment to argue some points in statistical mechanics, but real Maxwell's demons are coming closer and closer to becoming practical. Through the use of embedded sensors and agents, it is often conceivable to correct process problems right at the critical point of the process with minimum cost impact. Figure 1.2 diagrams how such a Maxwell's demon might work.

In spite of the incredible gains that have been made in the development of sensors, there have been even more miraculous advantages added through advancements in the analysis approaches behind these systems. Inspections that at one time could only be done by humans can now be accomplished by sophisticated cameras using pattern recognition systems. Inspections can be made simultaneously in a dozen different wavelengths and the information integrated in the blink of an eye. Learning algorithms and systems allow inspections to be integrated across time in an effective and intelligent fashion. Computers allow one to analyze and design acceptance sampling plans that exactly meet the process conditions while still providing needed guarantees. Fast statistical methods can be used on process inspection almost immediately to create adaptive control schemes and even change the process design in response to events.

The dramatic new power of inspection quality management comes directly from these tremendous increases in the speed, storage, and sophistication of sensors, measurements, and inspection processing systems. But improvements in these arenas would still be futile if they could not be integrated. This is the power and leverage that modern management needs to meet its current and future challenges.

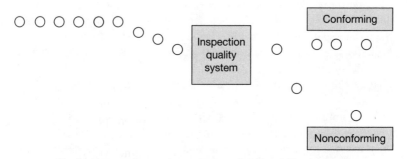

Production process produces a stream of products

Inspection quality system

Conforming

Nonconforming

The ideal inspection system acts as an intelligent filter to detect
and divert nonconformities based on their match to specifications.

Figure 1.2 Inspection systems as Maxwell's demon.

Production process as a sequence of steps that offer opportunity

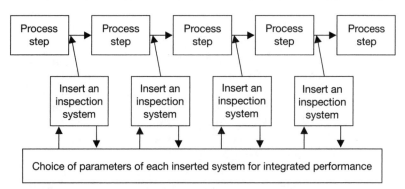

Figure 1.3 The integration of inspection systems.

Fundamentally, a manufacturer would like to manage its quality to meet its targets in a timely fashion with lowest cost. Inspection process quality management approaches propose that this can be accomplished by enacting a combination of adjustment policies that react quickly to process changes, control policies that create changes over a longer time, and product sorting that culls bad product. But such effective inspection processes require that one must stop placing the silos as has often been done in the past and instead force them to work together. There are methods to improve inspection components and effective approaches for combining the guarantees of each component into a system specifically targeted to the achievement of the quality objectives. These methods include statistical methods, operations research methods, and simulation. Figure 1.3 visualizes this integration of inspection systems.

THE PELLET CASE STUDY

Consider the example of a plastic pellet producer that sells bags of these items to toy manufacturers for use as flexible, lightweight fill material. Consider the specifics of one particular production line, line 10, which produces 1000 bags of these pellets each hour that it is operating at nominal machine cycle time. One specific pellet product code accounts for 40% of this company's entire yearly sales, so its successful production is critical to this concern's long-term health. Line 10 produces this critical product code 12 hours each day of a full seven day work week. The production cost per stockkeeping item, the bag of pellets, sells under contract for $10. It currently costs $8 to produce each bag, which yields a profit of $2 when things are running well. As stipulated by the contract, however, the customer may return any bags that are found defective at reception for a free replacement. In addition, if the average received nonconform rate exceeds 4% in any month, the customer may impose a 10¢ per bag penalty fee. In recent deliveries there have been lots of quality problems and much of the profit has been eroded.

The latest studies done on the process last month demonstrate that it is minimally capable with a Cp index (Ryan 1989) very close to 1.0. Due to pressure from a new vice president who was hired away from an automobile manufacturer, there has been a concerted effort over the last year to initiate and grow an active Six Sigma program (Pande 1992). This has not been easy, as the company has only a rather stagnant existing total quality management program that tends to rely exclusively on final product inspection to achieve its quality targets. The fledgling Six Sigma program is responsible for the capability study that was done on the process. The same program is trying to put together several projects targeted on reducing the variability of the process, and there is optimism running through the management circles that this effort will result in a big gain. But optimism alone does not always mean necessary funding and there is real doubt that such a beginner program can deliver the goods rapidly enough to make a fundamental difference. At best, this improvement effort will not come to fruition for two to three months and it is universally understood that there needs to be an effort to stem some of the financially penalizing quality problems immediately. Everyone working on the problem is a veteran of process improvement work, however, and they realize that temporary or short-term fixes have a high probability of turning into permanent fixtures when funding becomes an issue. No one would complain if the fix would be made permanent if it is necessary. The project team has developed three possible solutions that it sees as feasible. Consider Figure 1.4, which shows the pellet manufacturing process details.

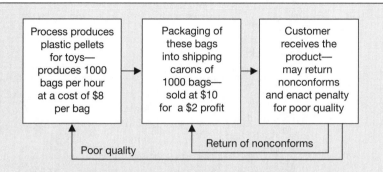

| Process produces plastic pellets for toys— produces 1000 bags per hour at a cost of $8 per bag | Packaging of these bags into shipping carons of 1000 bags— sold at $10 for a $2 profit | Customer receives the product— may return nonconforms and enact penalty for poor quality |

Poor quality

Return of nonconforms

Line 10 production line runs 12 hours per day seven days a week with a capability of 1.0 and has process improvement projects planned.

Figure 1.4 The plastic pellet manufacturing process.

An Acceptance Sampling Solution

The first option proposed is to install a standard acceptance sampling plan. This plan would be based on the definition of a batch as an entire shift's production of pellet bags or a total of 8000 bags. A system would be developed so that a random sample of 18 bags would be selected from each day's batch. This random sample would be routed from the production area to a dedicated inspection post that is located just before the packing area in which the bags are packaged into their final containers for delivery to the customer. The inspection that is to be performed at the inspection post is a destructive test. To perform this test, each sample bag is opened, a grab sample is taken from it, and a melting point test is applied. The estimate is that this inspection process will add an additional cost of about $1 per sampled bag.

According to the sampling plan logistics, if at least 1 of the 18 grab samples fails to pass the test criteria, then the entire batch, the entire 8000 bags for one day, are sent to an off-line area where additional tests are made to determine final distribution of that lot. If all of the 18 samples pass the test, then the rest of the lot, plus enough extra already tested good bags to meet the batch requirements, are packaged for delivery. Workers have some experience with sampling plans already existing in the company, so much of the workforce predicts minimal disruption if it is adopted. The project team itself believes the impact will be minimal because it can be applied entirely separately from the production process itself. See Figure 1.5 for a graphical representation of the acceptance sampling proposal.

A Fail-Safe or In-Line Inspection Solution

The second option that is suggested by the team is to install a new post into the production process itself that will serve as a sophisticated in-line inspection post much like a fail-safe. This is new process equipment that has just recently come onto the market. According to the manufacturer of the new post, it can be purchased and installed for a one-time investment of $1 million and there is a yearly maintenance cost of around $10,000 to ensure top performance. This preventive maintenance activity is to be scheduled once every quarter and requires that the production process be shut down for the four hours that are required for the maintenance activity. Right now the only team with the requisite knowledge to perform this maintenance is to be supplied from the vendor, but it is hoped that internal resources can be trained to pick up the responsibility with six months of installation.

There is some risk in that the device is new and does not yet have a long track record, but if it works according to the vendor's technical specifications, it should be quite effective. When operating

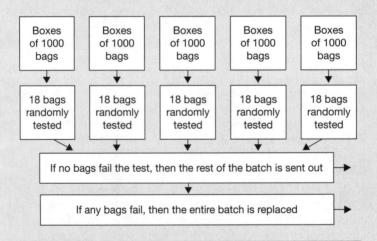

Figure 1.5 The acceptance sampling proposal.

under the process conditions for which it is designed, it is guaranteed to pick out 100% of the nonconforming pellets that are more than 2% over the sorting tolerance. To be able to provide this strong guarantee it does have a false reject rate of around 5% under these same conditions.

The recommended installation for this device is to locate it directly between the second and third steps in the current production process. Part of the high installation cost is the necessary rework to reorient these steps and create room for its installation. In addition to the downtime for installation and maintenance it is thought that there is likely to be a loss in cycle time, possibly at the 1% to 2% level. Delivery and installation will take at least one month and, of course, there will be the six months or so necessary to train the maintenance and production personnel. See Figure 1.6 for the details of the automatic in-line inspection system proposal.

An Auto-Quality Solution

The third option promulgated by the project team is to incorporate a small set of inspection and control duties into the production operators' work method. The operators, in addition to their

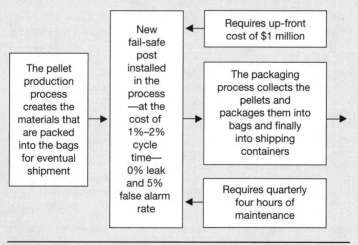

Figure 1.6 The fail-safe proposal.

duties of supervising the operation, would be required to make a visual inspection of the aspect of the product. Since this inspection would not have the specificity of the melting point test that is planned for the acceptance sampling approach, there would be a risk of more error. The project team estimates that a trained, alert operator would have about a 50% chance of picking up a product that is nonconforming by 5%. But, the point of inspection would be even earlier in the process than the fail-safe inspection and therefore would be opportune for sorting and controlling with maximal effect. The time that the operator needs to complete the inspection is small and should not detract too much from the time available to perform their manufacturing-related actions, at least under normal conditions when the process is running well.

It is clear that the operators will have to be trained to accomplish this task and a quality audit will have to be instituted in order to maintain their proficiency. There is some chance that the operators will resist the additional work since there is no corresponding increase in their pay. On the other hand, such an auto-quality system would certainly raise awareness in the operations staff about the importance of creating a quality culture. Overall, the project team thinks that this approach could have a very positive long-term payback for this reason alone. Figure 1.7 illustrates the auto-quality control proposal.

It should be clear from this example that it is not obvious how management should decide on which solution to adopt as a solution for their quality challenge. It seems critically important to

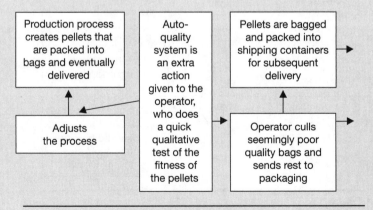

Figure 1.7 The auto-quality proposal.

first express the performances of each of these three solution options in equal terms and as closely as possible to estimate their expected gains. Quality costs in this system are determined by the appearance of nonconforming bags of pellets and the chance that they will be discovered by the customer in such levels that the quality penalty plays a major role. Production costs are determined by the known production costs and any associated cycle time impacts that the proposed solution might have. Additional costs include potential maintenance actions, training for affected personnel, and destructive inspection costs. There are also costs that are harder to assess, but no less important, such as the potential for unforeseen problems with the relatively new fail-safe equipment and the possible negativity of the operators if the auto-quality program is forced.

FOUR CRITICAL CHARACTERISTICS OF SOLUTIONS

At least four features should be thoroughly investigated for any proposed solution: statistical quality performance, cost of implementation, reliability of the system, and efficiency. The meaning of each of these features will be discussed in detail in later chapters, but for now it should be intuitively clear how they pertain to the pellet producer example. Statistical quality performance refers to the type of guarantee and its aptness to meet the requirements. Costs include all the one-time costs such as installation and the recurring costs of extra maintenance and supervisory activity. Reliability measures the quality of the performance through usage, especially the probability that the device or system would not be available when it is needed. The fourth feature, efficiency, is the relative work or difficulty that is required to make the inspection system perform.

The details of the evaluation of each of these characteristics will and should depend on the particular circumstances of the intended application, but no analysis of a proposed inspection solution should be considered complete until each of these characteristics is thoroughly investigated. A system must be strong in all of these areas to start strong and remain effective for the long haul. It must be able to meet these unanticipated needs as economically and simply as possible. One last thing to note is that some consideration should also be given to adaptability or extensibility of the inspection system. If one can easily extend the solution to a new situation in which more product is made or faster cycle times are available, then it would be considered extensible and adaptable to changes in process scope.

All of the proposed solutions are clearly inspection systems. Their basic action is the measurement of a product through a sensor or sense. In the case of the acceptance sampling system, the measurement is a complicated melting point test, which is interpreted by a human inspector. For the in-line fail-safe proposal, the inspection is automatic via spectral analysis and the decision to reject or accept is done by digital logics. For the auto-quality program, the inspection is visual and the interpretation is mediated by a human operator.

In each of these three inspection systems, the actions that can be taken predicated on the measurement results are also different. In the acceptance sampling systems, the basic decision is whether to block the lot and do additional testing. In the fail-safe situation, the decision is the rejection of individual bags of material. In the case of the auto-quality system, the decision appears to concern the culling of individual bags of pellets, but also some form of process feedback to reposition the process itself. This kind of variety in actions is quite usual for modern inspection systems of the type recommended in this book.

It is perhaps immediately clear that there are numerous issues dealing with the details of choosing specific parameters for each plan. This could be the number of samples per batch or even the batch size in the case of the acceptance sampling plan. It could be the tuning of the false-alarm rate versus specificity rate for the fail-safe. It could be the extent and immediacy of the operator training that is given to sustain the auto-quality program. In general, any inspection plan has numerous options of number of inspections, position of inspections, and type of inspection that are immediate. But there are other choices that can be just as important in the manner and extent of the treatment of these basic inspection inputs. This postprocessing of the raw inputs is really where much of the new power of modern inspections system stems. But it is one further step involving the choices of methods for integration of several inspection systems that opens up a whole world of new and powerful implementation options. Guidance and examples of these choices and these integration will be given in later chapters. In addition, the integration of these inspection systems into an overall Six Sigma, lean manufacturing (Liker 1997), or other total quality management program will be discussed in the penultimate chapter.

In most companies, these activities will be done at the management level. It is management's role to guide this integration of the different quality approaches and their evolution from existing systems. Fortunately, this plays to the strength of the effective modern manager. Good managers

(Bennis 2004) are especially adept at choosing and adapting strategies to their real-world situations. For example, if they can achieve more by assuming an autocratic, parental role, good managers will push this aspect. If they sense that the environment favors a cooperative, lateral organization, then they become accomplished mentors and coaches. Of course every manager may not be equally capable of playing all these required roles, so it is really management, generically, that must exhibit these characteristics. There will always be significant challenges in a given situation, but the information given in this book combined with some of the reference material should be sufficient, with practice, to enable a good manager to apply this integrated approach to inspection quality management correctly and effectively.

Chapter 1 Value Propositions

1. Sensors and measurements are the sources for inspections.

2. Inspections are drivers of process or product improvement.

3. Inspections systems include sampling, control, and adjustment.

4. Inspections must have adequate quality, cost, reliability, and efficiency.

5. Integration of inspections system is the key to successful implementation.

2

The Measurement of Inspection Performance

STATISTICAL QUALITY PERFORMANCE

It is important to repeat that the there are at least four critical features that should be investigated for any inspection quality system: statistical quality performance, cost, reliability, and efficiency. The remainder of this chapter will now examine each of these features in great detail with examples of how they might be evaluated.

It is said that quality, like beauty, is in the eye of the beholder. There are probably as many different definitions of quality as there are persons who have tried to define it. According to the dictionary, *quality* refers to a feature that distinguishes or identifies something. In a manufacturing or commercial enterprise this distinguishing feature is often more narrowly defined as the degree or grade of excellence (American Heritage Dictionary 1985). Other definitions emphasize conformance to specifications or fitness for use. Most of the definitions are consistent in their insistence that whatever quality is, it surely has at least four properties. First, it must depend to some extent on how well the product or service conforms to its specifications, in other words, how fit it is for its intended use. Second, it must depend on the user's perception of its usefulness or fitness for use. A third necessary characteristic of quality is that it is multidimensional. Its impact may be approximated by a single monetary value, but this approximation is understood to be a complex combination of several separate performance features. The fourth characteristic of quality that most experts stress is its dynamic nature. It can change in time and, sometimes, can change quite rapidly. Although changes in time are the most usual ways in which the quality can change, it can also vary as a function of influential background variables, including influences from competition and cooperation in the marketplace. Since quality is often associated with a subjective human appreciation, then none of these characteristics should be all that surprising. Many of these characteristics are simply part and parcel of any activity that relies on human judgment.

Because quality depends on the user and can change through time, generally it can only be measured practically by statistical measures. The fundamental concept lying behind the evaluation of quality seems to be the placement of products with inherently different quality into usage by users each with unique perceptions. Each of these users combines the multiple product performance features of each product into a single perception of quality at the moment of use. This opinion may change a moment later when another product is viewed in competition or the user's attention is distracted by some other concern. Thus quality is really a statistical property of the product over the user population and its changing characteristics. Overall quality is directly determined by the distribution of quality over a population of users. Distributions such as these are often summarized to a few numbers such as mean, variance, maximum value, and other statistics to enable easier manipulation.

THE TEXTBOOK PUBLISHING CASE STUDY

Imagine that you are a publisher of textbooks for middle school mathematics classes. How would you determine the quality of the product, the textbook, that you deliver? First of all, you realize that there are multiple dimensions to the usefulness of the textbook. There is the accuracy of the content, its conformance to state standards, its readability, the number of practice problems, the visual impact of the text, and the sheer weight of the tome. Each of these features could be evaluated separately and then combined into an overall suitability or quality function. Then there is the fact that if this textbook is purchased, it will be used for all eighth grade mathematics classes in the entire school district or even state. This means that a variety of students, teachers, and parents will experience the textbook, and each one will have an opinion of its quality. The evaluation of quality will also depend on how long the evaluation period is. The customer opinion may change drastically if the evaluation period is one week or one semester or the entire academic year. A new textbook might be evaluated highly at first just because it is new and students are excited. By mid-year, the students may be lost and transfer their frustration with the class to the textbook and quality would dip. Finally, at year-end, the students may sort out in their evaluation of the textbook in the same way as their final grade in the class. Of course the inherent characteristic of the book itself also impacts this evaluation; a book with inadequate coverage will seldom be rated highly in quality. If any attempt is made to evaluate the quality of the textbook, it will certainly involve a sample of student and teacher opinion, and a statistical summary will be necessary. See Figure 2.1 for a diagram of the situation.

Table 2.1 shows an example of what a survey of 100 students could produce on three measures of performance and on an overall quality rating.

Once these quality performance characteristics are defined and evaluated, they must be converted into a format that can be compared on a fair basis with the other features such as cost. This is not always possible and can be awkward even in cases where it is possible. There are ways to handle totally independent features, such as multiple criteria decision making (MCDM) (Morrice 1998), but it is far easier to work with equivalent criteria. One way in which to do this in the quality arena is through the use of quality loss functions.

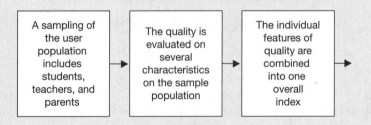

Figure 2.1 The textbook evaluation process.

Table 2.1 The results of a survey of 100 students on three measures.

Measure	Sample size	Mean	Standard deviation
Conformance	100	4.61	2.87
Readability	100	4.57	1.92
Usability	100	4.84	2.97

Quality Loss Function

It is possible to track the exact costs related to nonquality (Campanella 1999), but this requires a good deal of effort and lots of updating to keep it current. Another disadvantage of this exhaustive approach is that it often underestimates the value of intangible costs. A more subtle problem is that this approach can lead to the conclusion that there is best value of quality, equal to the loss. This violates the spirit of continuous improvement (Bisgaard 2004), which would conclude that one never reaches good enough.

Taguchi (Ryan 1989) takes an alternative approach that focuses on the potential losses due to nonquality. The quality loss is taken to be the function that combines the distribution of produced products and the loss as a function of distance from target. Because this curve should change for each quality dimension, for each consumer, and for different periods of evaluation, it is simply a useful approximation. Since it is an approximation, it usually does no harm to simplify this loss function further by assuming it is a simple quadratic with the minimum at the target. There is no strict requirement that this kind of curve be used for the loss function, but it is the usual formulation. One must be careful to calibrate it with realistic costs when one plans to combine and compare these costs to internal costs. It is adequate for setting directions and for relative evaluations of alternatives, and can correlate with measures of company market share (Rust 1999).

APPLYING THE TAGUCHI LOSS FUNCTION TO THE PELLET CASE STUDY

As an example of how this might work, consider the bags of plastic pellets in the case study from Chapter 1. If we apply the Taguchi loss function to this situation, we would first start with drawing a loss function. Since this example deals with only one specification, the one measured by the melting test, and one corporate customer, it is much simpler than a full-blown situation. The cost evaluated by the Taguchi loss function is the potential loss that is expected if the nonconforming product was delivered to the consumer. Because these losses are only potential, they can be avoided by inspection or process improvements when actual shipments are made.

It is assumed that the loss is zero, or at least minimum, when the delivered product characteristic is perfectly on target. It is further assumed that if the product characteristic is equal to the tolerance, then the loss will be twice the selling value, or $20 in this case. If this tolerance is at 20% of target value, the resulting loss function could look like the one displayed in Figure 2.2.

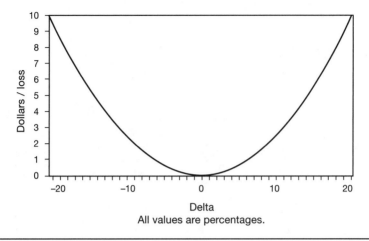

Figure 2.2 The true quality loss function.

This function approximates the total quality loss of a product that is experienced by a customer if the product is delivered at a particular quality. One of its major applications is that it can be easily applied to measure the impact of quality management alternatives. To do this one must combine the loss function with the distribution of quality for delivered bags. In the pellet example, the capability of the process was recently estimated to be 1.00. Such a distribution of normal values could look as the histogram in Figure 2.3 if it had a mean of 101 melt point units (mpu) and a standard deviation of 1 mpu. A target of 100 mpu would then yield an estimate of Cp = 1.00 as given in the example.

This histogram shows how many product bags should have various meltpoint values. Each particular meltpoint value then can be combined with the loss curve to estimate a potential loss. If we continue this process for a large number of simulated products, we will obtain a distribution of losses. As an example, consider what a sample of 10,000 simulated loss values could look like, as appears in Figure 2.4. Table 2.2 shows the summary statistics which characterize this sample.

The average loss of the current process is 4.96¢ per item. This loss should be interpreted as an approximate potential loss if there is no additional work done to prevent the poorer products from being delivered. The losses will not, in general, correspond to real accountable costs for a concern unless special care is taken to calibrate the computation to real costs. But even without this complicated calibration, the loss computed in this manner can be suitable for proper evaluation of project and improvement alternatives. The

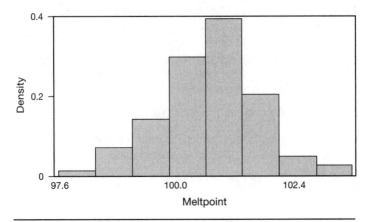

Figure 2.3 The distribution of pellet melting points.

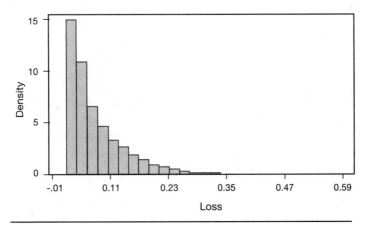

Figure 2.4 The distribution of pellet losses.

Table 2.2 The summary statistics for this distribution of pellet losses.

Moments			
N	10,000.0000	Sum Wgts	10,000.0000
Mean	0.0496	Sum	495.8430
Std Dev	0.0604	Variance	0.0037
Skewness	2.2166	Kurtosis	7.3318
USS	61.0961	CSS	36.5100
CV	121.8663	Std Mean	0.0006

loss function promotes a simple, objective way in which to evaluate the value of any action that prevents the products that cause high loss from being delivered to the customer. Alternatively, actions that have effects on the shape and extent will also have a positive value that can be measured through the loss function in this way.

Evaluation of the Fail-Safe Losses

Consider the impact of installing the fail-safe on the quality losses. The installation of the fail-safe costs $1,000,000 in a one-shot installation with a $10,000 yearly upkeep fee. It provides a 100% guarantee that all products beyond $+/-2\%$ from target are removed. Pictorially, the impact of activating the in-line inspection can be displayed as in Figure 2.5. Notice that the truncation of the distribution is abrupt on the upper part of the curve.

Note that there is still some quality loss attributed to products with meltpoints that do not match the target value even though their meltpoint values are within the tolerances. These losses are probably real in the sense that customers will experience poorer performances in these situations, but they would not be traceable from actual quality loss records or warranty claims. It is straightforward to simulate the estimated loss under the scenario with the active fail-safe by simply screening out the losses that were originally due to these aberrant values. Based on the new computation, the average loss per item is only 2.65¢, or, at most, 3¢ with the fail-safe. This implies a savings of 2¢ per bag in the fail-safe over the baseline scenario in which there is no inspection system in application. Since the installation price of the fail-safe is $1 million, it would take 1,000,000 times 20 to equal 20 million items to break

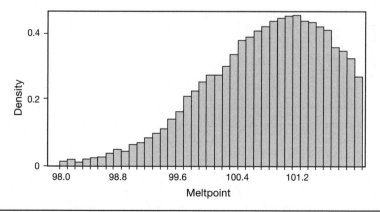

Figure 2.5 Distribution of melting points for the fail-safe.

even just using installation costs to judge the impact. Since this process makes roughly 140,000 items per week, the fail-safe would pay for itself in 142 weeks or about 2¾ years. Of course, there may be other costs such as maintenance and training that should also be considered, but these will be ignored for the present since this is not meant to be a complete course in project evaluation methodology. Figure 2.6 shows the expected loss distribution after the fail-safe is installed. Table 2.3 shows the summary statistics for this expected loss distribution.

Evaluation of Acceptance Sampling Losses

The proposed batch attribute acceptance sampling plan gives a guarantee on the average outgoing quality in similar way to that of the fail-safe approach. What is not expressed in most discussions of sampling plans is

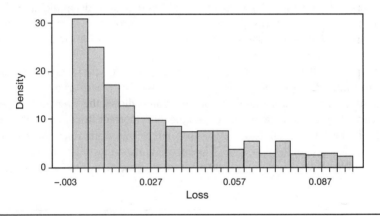

Figure 2.6 Effect of the fail-safe on the loss.

Table 2.3 Summary statistics of losses of the fail-safe.

Moments			
N	832.0000	Sum Wgts	832.0000
Mean	0.0265	Sum	22.0067
Std Dev	0.0260	Variance	0.0007
Skewness	1.0039	Kurtosis	0.0106
USS	1.1439	CSS	0.5618
CV	98.3038	Std Mean	0.0009

the effect on the distribution's variability. But this can be simulated in a straightforward, if slightly more complicated, way. Now the simulation logic must mimic the batches and the action of sampling that is done. It must also mimic the action of 100% rectification in the case of rejected lots. If the population is taken to be the same normal distribution with mean equals 101 mpu and standard deviation equals 1 mpu, then we can estimate a percentage nonconforming to equal a 2% nonconform rate. Roughly, this equates to limits of +3% and −3% on the meltpoint distribution. This is displayed in Figure 2.7.

This distribution of meltpoints can be coupled with the loss function to create a distribution of potential losses, as given in Figure 2.8, and a set of summary statistics as in Table 2.4. Note that the average loss is expected to be 4.29¢ per bag for a savings of roughly 1¢ per bag versus the baseline process without inspection. Of course, this guarantee has to be paid for with additional samples. The size of this sampling cost will be discussed further, but for now simply observe the expected loss distribution of the pellet process under the implementation of the proposed acceptance sampling plan.

Evaluation of the Auto-Quality Losses

The third proposal, the auto-quality program, allows the operator to take samples immediately and adjust the process to correct them. The estimate of effectiveness of this proposal is to catch 50% of those bags that are

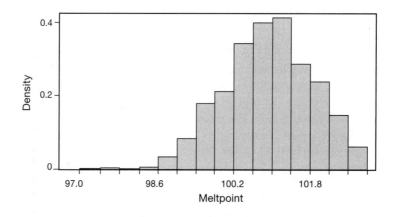

Figure 2.7 Distribution of melting points under the acceptance sampling plan.

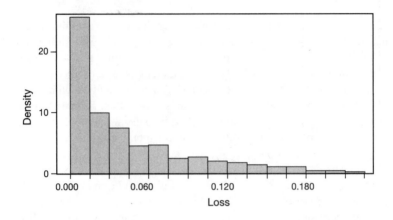

Figure 2.8 Loss distribution under acceptance sampling.

Table 2.4 Summary statistics of loss under acceptance sampling.

Moments			
N	976.0000	Sum Wgts	976.0000
Mean	0.0429	Sum	41.8373
Std Dev	0.0477	Variance	0.0023
Skewness	1.4028	Kurtosis	1.3362
USS	4.0091	CSS	2.2157
CV	111.2083	Std Mean	0.0015

more than $+/-2\%$ from target. This effect can also be described by a simulation of parts from the process. The simulation begins with the generation of 10,000 bags that fall according to the full meltpoint distribution. The values that fall outside of the $+/-2\%$ limits are identified and, at random, rejected at a 50% rate. The resulting product distribution could look like Figure 2.9.

Marrying this to the loss function in a similar way to that in which the fail-safe and the acceptance sampling plans were evaluated leads to a loss distribution, as displayed in Figure 2.10. The summary behavior given in Table 2.5 shows that the average loss is now 4.5¢ per bag for a savings of 0.5¢ over the baseline conditions that reflect the absence of any type of inspection quality system.

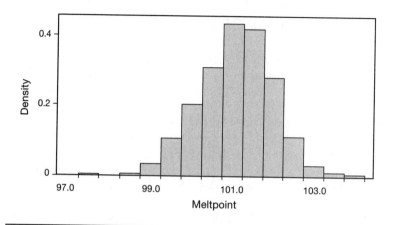

Figure 2.9 The distribution of melting points under the auto-quality proposal.

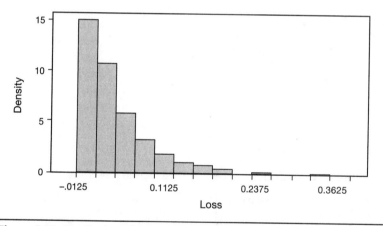

Figure 2.10 Distribution of losses under the auto-quality proposal.

Table 2.5 Summary statistics of losses under auto-quality.

Moments			
N	913.0000	Sum wgts	913.0000
Mean	0.0379	Sum	34.6118
Std dev	0.0477	Variance	0.0023
Skewness	2.5661	Kurtosis	9.3645
USS	3.3883	CSS	2.0762
CV	125.8578	Std mean	0.0016

COST OF INSPECTION

There are many costs related to an investment proposal, and this book will not try to replace the good cost-accounting and cost-engineering references that are available. Instead the focus will be on the costs associated directly with inspection quality systems. Most costs associated with inspection systems are divided among four broad categories: (1) fixed costs that are insensitive to the number of measurements, (2) fixed costs per unit that are proportional to the number of measurements, (3) variable costs that change in a nonproportional way to the number of measurements, and (4) costs that vary in ways that are not directly related to the number of measurements.

Within these four categories, the particular components of the cost will vary with each application, but here is a list of the most common of such components:

1. Cost of equipment purchase or modification

2. Cost of personnel changes

3. Cost of training for operations

4. Cost of training for maintenance

5. Cost of training for other support personnel

6. Installation costs

7. Impacts on the efficiency of the production process

8. Impacts on the reliability of the production process

9. Impacts on personnel morale

10. Opportunity loss

Example of Cost for the Three Pellet Case Study Proposals

The fail-safe costs include a fixed purchase price of $1 million, recurring annual maintenance fees of $10,000, plus whatever loss of production occurs. The production cycle time loss that is anticipated is expressed as a percentage of current production amounts so the loss could grow or shrink if different cycle times are used. As an example of a realistic estimate of this loss one might use 3% of every dollar earned in sales. Another cost associated with the fail-safe or in-line inspection post is generated by the training and possible hiring of maintenance personnel to service this new component, probably on the order of $10,000 per year. There would probably be a huge opportunity loss associated with this proposal as $1 million in capital costs would probably slow or abort other potential projects that should be considered as well.

The costs associated with the acceptance sampling plan are more subtle in nature than those of the fail-safe. First, there is cost to be paid for setting up the new inspection posts. This cost includes equipment such as scissors to open the bags and the melting test apparatus, perhaps represented as a value of $200 per post. Then there are possible personnel costs due to the demand for either new staffing or at least a transfer of duties for current staff, perhaps 2 to 3 full-time positions. And there is training for this inspection staff and probably for audit personnel as well, perhaps hidden in their normal personal development costs. Then there is the cost due to the destructive sampling process itself with a fixed cost of 18 bags times $1, and a variable cost depending on how many extra cleansing samples are necessary. The details are given in Chapter 5, but the curve in Figure 2.11 shows the relationship between the produced quality and this variable sampling cost. Reading the curve, we expect an additional 50¢ per bag on average coming from these variable costs.

The auto-quality program has costs related to training of personnel in the new methods and perhaps some equipment to support it. This might be 0.5 to 1 full-time position. There is a risk of production slowdown due to the double duty of the operator under this system, but this seems to be

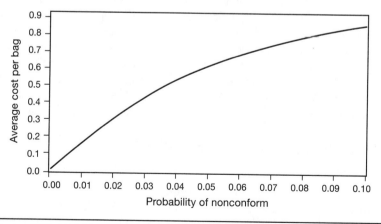

Figure 2.11 Variable cost per bag under the acceptance sampling plan.

a small amount, perhaps 0.1% of each bag. And there is probably some personnel or payroll work to be done to gain the support of the operators as they take on more work and responsibility. This could be significant if pay rate hikes are required. There is also likely to be additional training and work required for the quality staff to track and audit the program, but again this might be covered by normal operating expenditures. There is also hidden cost due to mistaken adjustments of the process made by the operator in attempts to correct a nonexistent deviation. This could be large, but given the capability of the process would not likely add more than 1% to the manufacturing cost.

THE RELIABILITY PERFORMANCE OF INSPECTIONS

It is also important to be able to characterize and control the reliability performance of the acceptance quality management inspection. *Reliability* is the probability that a device or system will be adequately functioning at a specified time (Henley 1981). Often reliability is referred to as quality through time (Meeker 2000). The reliability of an inspection or inspection process can be evaluated in identical ways as might a piece of production or manufacturing equipment.

Reliability, because it refers to a probability, should be evaluated via proper statistical procedures. For example, we can put a sampling of similar inspection devices under test and then track the failure time for each component. Failure is a point at which the performance of the device does not meet requirements. Some systems may fail catastrophically, which makes the evaluation of failure much easier than when it is simply a more subtle performance deterioration that marks the failure. With a proper number of samples, and hence failure times, it is possible to estimate a curve showing the expected relationship between time in service for a device and the probability of failure, as in Figure 2.12. Based on this chart, we would have only 15% reliability if the required service life was 10,000 hours.

Reliability Assessment for the Pellet Case Study Proposals

For a unique machine or process component like the fail-safe device, it is difficult for the purchaser to independently test its reliability, so often guarantees from the supplier must be used. According to the vendor's description, the device will perform at its stated performance if one does

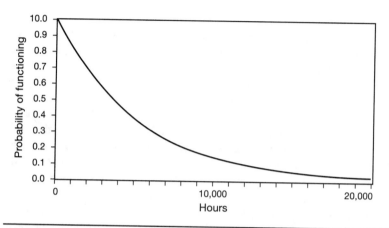

Figure 2.12 Reliability of device versus hours of operation.

the required maintenance. But what if the maintenance is delayed or done poorly? This will likely affect the reliability negatively and we should consider this effect. In addition to problems affecting the in-line inspection device itself, there may be additional failures in supporting systems that could also prevent proper performance. For example, there might not be a trained technician available when needed and the machine, and the process, might be idle for some time. The fail-safe system is apparently a complex piece of equipment with process parts, measurement parts, and postprocessing parts, each of which could have vastly different reliabilities. It is also clear that the guarantees are closely correlated with maintenance of standard operating conditions. If the process changes significantly, then the reliability may consequently be affected for good or bad.

The acceptance sampling plan reliability can better be estimated within the company itself. For example, the inspectors might deteriorate in their performance to such an extent that the entire inspection system fails. Many visual inspections have error rates as high at 10% in both false negatives and false positives. Also the test equipment might malfunction. Perhaps there is historical data from which it can be estimated that a breakdown occurs every 2500 tests on average. Then replacement parts better be ready as needed to prevent a bottleneck from forming in inspection. There might also be problems with delivery systems and sampling methods with this approach.

The auto-quality system is dependent on the operators and thus might have the same reliability issues as the sampling inspection posts. Sometimes there might be a complete breakdown if an operator leaves the post for an unexcused emergency or simply to visit the break room at the wrong time. Or the failure might be more subtle, as when a deterioration results when the inspector gets too busy with production issues to do the inspection job properly. The reliability can be estimated by watching operator routines and monitoring their behavior over time. In this case, it is found that they are only 80% reliable over a month period. This reliability is found to depend on many things including the amount of training received; the motivation of the operators, and the adequacy of the auditing system that is done. In this situation there may not be a catastrophic failure potential, but it is likely that the inspection performance will suffer. Most likely these problems will manifest themselves in the making of more mistakes, the skipping of samples, or in the improper selection of samples in the first place.

There are many good tools of both elementary and sophisticated nature that can be applied to the study of reliability and its improvement. One such tool, failure modes and effects analysis (FMEA) (Stamatis 1995) should be mentioned in particular since it is of such wide usage in quality management circles. FMEA is a systematic procedure in which the experts of the system try to exhaustively list each possible failure mode and then assign a risk rating to that mode's effects. Typically, this risk rating has two components: the severity of the effect and its probability of occurrence. In some systems, there is a moderating impact of detectability that is evaluated in addition to these other elements. FMEA can be applied with good effect on acceptance quality management inspections as well.

The application of FMEA to the auto-quality program might result in a listing like the one shown in Table 2.6. Alongside the listing are two other columns showing the ratings given by team of experts as to the severity and probability of occurrence on a subjectively-based scale from 1 to 10. The final column is the product of the two risk columns and can be used to prioritize problems and remedial actions. A guideline often used in determining

Table 2.6 FMEA analysis of the auto-quality program.

Source	Severity	Frequency	Priority rating
No operator	10	1	10
Slow operator	5	1	5
Operator mistake	1	5	5
No product	10	1	10
Bad product view	1	10	10
Speed of post	10	10	100
Malformed product	10	8	80

which failure modes that are mandatory to fix is to choose those items with priority rating of 80 or above.

Based on this analysis, work should be done to improve the speed of post effect and the effect of malformed product. Of course, other considerations such as cost and feasibility can also influence the final decision about where constrained resources will be used first.

THE EFFICIENCY OF INSPECTIONS

Alongside the quality, cost, and reliability dimensions that can be associated with an inspection, there is a fourth dimension of efficiency. Although sometimes this can be expressed as a cost, it is more useful to separate the flow characteristics of the inspection procedure. There are many and varied approaches that can be profitably applied to this endeavor, including:

1. Theory of constraints

2. Lean manufacturing

3. Optimization programming approaches

4. Heuristic methods

5. Simulation methods

Lean manufacturing (George 2002), for example, focuses on the minimum times needed for various substeps of the inspection process and compares these to the actual times to reduce non-value-added processing time or the TAKT index. This approach then implements various scheduling tools to change from a push operation in which there may be much waiting stock produced to a pull system in which only that which is needed is manufactured. Theory of constraints (Goldratt 1990) emphasizes a management program in which one identifies process bottlenecks, eliminates them, and then iterates to the new bottlenecks.

Efficiency Assessment for the Pellet Case Study Proposals

As an example of how this might work for the acceptance sampling program, consider the sampling process in more detail. First, the sample is selected from the process stream, apparently just prior to shipping. From the description of the process this must amount to selecting a box, opening it, selecting some pieces, and testing these. The test procedure itself probably includes steps of sample preparation, sample treatment, interpreting results, and recording results. If all the selected samples pass, then there is an action to bypass the rest of the lot. If the samples fail then there is another procedure to transfer the whole batch to the inspection post from their storage in warehouse or terminal. The lean manufacturing approach could list these steps and attempt to estimate the minimum and actual times associated with each step. Such a list might look like the one in Table 2.7.

Work could be concentrated on the steps with the bigger differences between the actual and required times such as select box, select pieces, and sample preparation steps in the inspection cycle. Or one might attempt to eliminate whole steps that are now considered essential, but could be questioned. For example, if the boxes are left unsealed until after the inspection post, then one could eliminate the open box step completely. Whatever the details of the particular process are, the important point is that at least these four essential properties should be investigated and characterized.

Table 2.7 Required and actual times for acceptance sampling.

Process step	Required time	Actual time
Select box	2 minutes	6 minutes
Open box	1 minute	1 minute
Select pieces	3 minutes	15 minutes
Sample preparation	10 minutes	15 minutes
Sample treatment	2 minutes	2 minutes
Interpret results	2 minutes	5 minutes
Record results	1 minute	2 minutes
Pass lot	1 minute	1 minute
Reject lot	1 minute	1 minute
Cleansing sample	3 minutes	6 minutes

Chapter 2 Value Propositions

1. Inspections must have adequate quality, cost, reliability, and efficiency.

2. Quality can be measured by Taguchi loss functions.

3. Cost should include well-defined cost components.

4. Reliability is the probability the inspection will perform at a given time.

5. Efficiency can be evaluated through failure modes and effects (FMEA).

3

The Fundamental Importance of Sensors

SENSORS AS SOURCES OF MEASUREMENT

As emphasized in Chapters 1 and 2, the engine of product and process continuous improvement is the inspection. Without a critical examination there can be no action, be it a continuous adjustment, a less frequent control action, or an erratic process improvement. The inspection is dependent on measurements that are obtained through either a sensor or a sense. No matter how sophisticated or powerful the data treatment and analysis are, their results are constrained by the characteristics of these sensors. A sensor or a sense is a component that can interact with a process and produce a meaningful output. The most common example of a sensor is any one of the human senses: sight, hearing, smell, taste, touch. For example, hearing is mediated by the ear with its auditory canal, drum, anvil, stirrups, and special fluid. A sensor is almost identical to a measurement device, which is a system whose function is to interact with another process and produce an output that can be used to characterize the state of the system in question (AIAG 2002). A sensor is best understood as either a simple measurement system or as the front end of a more complex measurement system. Modern sensors come in a bewildering array of types, sizes, and sophistication. The following is a partial listing of available sensors:

1. Unaided human sight, hearing, smell, touch, and taste

2. Enhanced human sight, hearing, smell, touch, and taste

3. Electronic sensors for electromagnetic spectrum

4. Electronic sensors for pressure

5. Electronic sensors for temperature

6. Electronic sensors for radioactivity

7. Electronic sensors for chemical reactions

8. Physical devices for pressure

9. Physical devices for temperature

10. Human aesthetic perceptions

11. Computer counting

12. Density or gray scale changes

Each of these can be used separately or in conjunction with other sensors. These combinations can be connected in series, in parallel, or in any complicated array. In remote sensing applications, it is common to build sensor arrays that have multiple sensors, perhaps with each sensor measuring a different physical property, arranged in a specific structure to provide the best sensor coverage of an area. More and more, sensors are equipped with some internal processing power to become what is termed a "smart sensor." Any list is necessarily outdated immediately due to the incredible rate of new development and improvement of new sensors. They are becoming faster, cheaper, more energy efficient, and more intelligent with each passing day.

As manufacturing equipment is updated, there are almost always new sensors implemented to make measurements at that point in the process. Most of the time this information is only utilized for start-up and maintenance purposes, but many progressive companies are also collecting this embedded inspection information and sending it to linked computers or data warehouses where further processing can be done. This kind of post-processing is a very powerful enhancement for the general approach of inspection quality management.

Another development in sensor application technology is the mobile drone or unguided monitoring system (Kennedy 2001). This is most often applied in aerial surveillance applications where a great deal of territory, often hostile, must be covered, but there is potential for manufacturing as well. For example, one might have a sensor fixed in a guide path positioned above a long roll of extruded material. One could have multiple fixed position sensors at spaced intervals measuring temperature of this roll, but one could also have this mobile sensor fly a specified or random path to selectively sample, and perhaps adaptively sample, the temperature across the roll. Sensors tend to be very inexpensive so one need not think too hard about this trade-off, but, of course, infrastructure restrictions should be used where possible. Some application modalities of sensors are:

1. In isolated application
2. In series with other applications
3. In parallel with other applications
4. In complex dependencies with other applications
5. Smart sensors
6. Sensors in networks
7. Sensors as agents

IMAGE ENHANCEMENTS

The basic sensor properties put constraints on the eventual use of the information but this does not mean that powerful enhancement is worthless. In fact, for many systems it is the rapidity of the sensor measurements that enables the treatment to make them more useful as a set than would be judged based on the inherent value of any single measurement. A laser measurement (Carroll 1970) of the width of a plastic strip may not have great measurement performance for each individual reading, but one can take thousands of measurements in the same time as would be required to obtain a single measurement by hand. Often the use of simple statistical averaging is used on each set of multiple measurements to make the inspection quite powerful. Statistical averaging can improve measurement performance by a hundredfold in a relatively short time period without physical contact with the product. Vision and camera systems can be used in the same way and to the same advantages as laser systems.

THE LASER CASE STUDY

An individual laser measurement may, because of angular reflection, offset, and resolution, have an appreciable measurement error on each single sensor reading. In an application in which one is measuring the length of a metal strip, the laser sensor might be able to measure accurately with no systematic offset but with a standard deviation of 1 mm. If the laser can take 100 independent measurements per second, then postprocessing can average them and report this average as the single length measurement. This average will have much less variation in most cases, probably on the order of one tenth of the individual reading, or 0.1 mm in this example. This simple data treatment can enhance the inspection ten fold. And most commercial laser-based systems are much more sophisticated in removing outliers (Barnett 1984) and accounting for cross correlation (Ott 1984) so they can do even better. See Figure 3.1 for an illustration of a laser measurement system.

The amount of treatment that can be applied is limited primarily by the time available to take action and the format of the sensor output. A human-enabled measurement almost always has to be recorded manually into some electronic media before it can be treated in any sophisticated way. And if the original sensor is a photographic image or a chemical test, it can easily eat up an hour or more of actual time to process it. So the ideal inspection quality management system will likely have many sensors, many layers of enhancement, and some kind of final postprocessing to actually produce the action. This action can be on the product for continuous product improvement or on the process for continuous process improvement, The consistent objective is to provide better outgoing quality feasibly and at minimal cost. Figure 3.2 tries to illustrate what such an ideal system of sensors might look like.

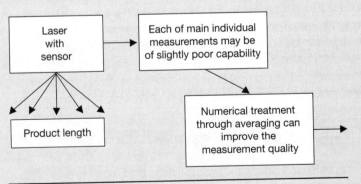

Figure 3.1 The laser measurement sensor system.

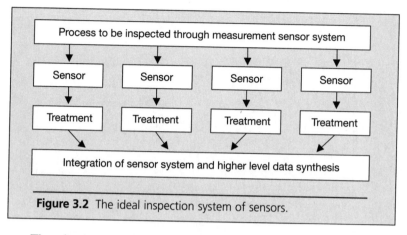

Figure 3.2 The ideal inspection system of sensors.

There is no reason that the enhancement needs to be based on a single measurement. For example, one might take a series of equally spaced measurements and then convert to Fourier frequencies (Schwartz 1975). It is the processed harmonic content that can then be used for the inspection decision. And with today's software, the sophistication of this treatment can be quite extensive. With data warehouses (English 1999) and expert systems (Harmon 1985) the basic information content contained in the sensor output can be treated with the best of hard-won knowledge. All of these technological enhancements directly impact the value of inspections in today's quality manufacturing. The characterization of the performance of acceptance quality management systems will be based on all these possible sensory and enhancement systems as they are treated as a single input to the acceptance sampling, auto-quality, or fail-safe procedure.

THE FOURIER FREQUENCY CASE STUDY

In automobile tire inspections, it is common to measure the forces that the tire produces when pushed on by a load. This is done by sampling several hundred equally spaced values around the tire circumference with the same sensor. Postprocessing then computes the discrete Fourier transform of these points to produce estimates of the first harmonic effect. It is this first harmonic estimate that is treated as the basic inspection of the tire performance. The values, magnitudes, and azimuths can then be used to trigger direct product improvement activities such as rectification or to trigger process adjustment and control purposes. Figure 3.3 shows the individual measurements and the fitted Fourier first harmonic.

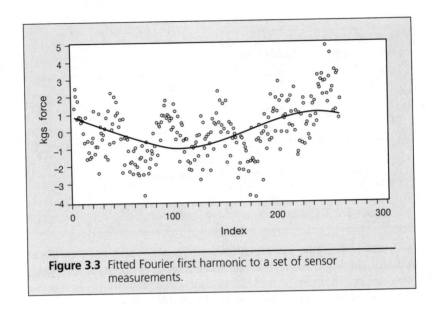

Figure 3.3   Fitted Fourier first harmonic to a set of sensor measurements.

MEASUREMENT SYSTEM ANALYSIS

Because inspections are sensors plus enhancements, they must meet the requirements of a good measurement system. A *measurement system* is the totality of all devices, methods, personnel, and reference materials that affect the result of the measurement (AIAG 2000). The first step in an adequate measurements system analysis is to make a list of all things that can affect the measurement to any significant degree. Then an attempt should be made to estimate each of these impacts. If one succeeds in estimating these component effects as standard deviations, then it is often possible to assume that they combine as independent quantities, namely as the sum of their squares. The square root of this total is called the *total uncertainty* and often one takes + and − 2 times this total uncertainty as an interval expressing the uncertainty around any individual reading. Table 3.1 shows an example of an uncertainty analysis. The combined system uncertainty is then computed as the square root of the sum of the squared uncertainty components and is equal to 5.66 grams. Finally, an interval is computed as + or − 2 times this system uncertainty, and the total uncertainty is then quoted as +/− 11.32 grams.

In many manufacturing concerns, there are literally thousands of measurement devices in use at any given time. So the work involved with a full uncertainty analysis is prohibitive. A shortened uncertainty analysis is known as measurement systems analysis (MSA) and concentrates

Table 3.1 An uncertainty analysis of a sensor.

Uncertainty source	Type	Uncertainty component
Sample aging	Test	1.1 grams
Sample cut	Test	5.0 grams
Sample handling	Expert opinion	2.3 grams
Sample placement	Expert opinion	0.5 grams
Traceability	External reference	0.04 grams
Calibration	External reference	0.12 grams
Operator training	Test	0.30 grams
Size of sample	Test	0.35 grams
Shape of sample	Expert opinion	0.21 grams
Environmental state	Expert opinion	0.06 grams

on just two of the many potential impacts: operator reproducibility and device repeatability.

This simplification is justified by the fact that for many measurement systems these two components dominate the other sources. See Figure 3.4 for a schematic of MSA's restrictions.

Specifically, *repeatability* is defined as the variation due to repeat measurements taken by the same operator on the same product. The thinking is that this variation captures mainly the effect of the device or sensor itself. This may or may not be true, depending on the stability of the product and any changes in background conditions. Figure 3.5 illustrates the concept of repeatability for a measurement system.

Reproducibility is defined as the variation between the average of repeat measurements made by different operators on the same parts. That is, each operator makes multiple measurements on the same part. Then the averages of these repeats are computed for each part-operator combination. Then the differences in these averages, aligned by part, are compared to arrive at a standard deviation representing the operator reproducibility. This can be affected by the stability of the products, the size of repeatability variation, and the consistency of the operator behavior. Figure 3.6 illustrates this concept in which each curve represents a different operator.

A complete MSA also checks the *resolution* of the device, which is the least increment that is distinguishable in a reading. For a ruler, this would be the incremental markings imprinted on the surface. It is also good to check various other properties of the measurements including their normality, their stability, and their effective resolution. Figure 3.7 illustrates the concept of resolution.

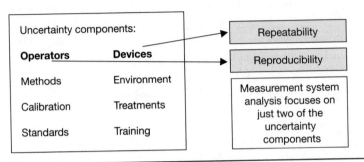

Figure 3.4 The relationship between uncertainty and measurement analysis.

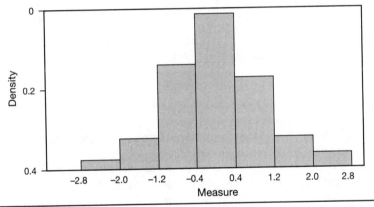

Figure 3.5 The concept of repeatability.

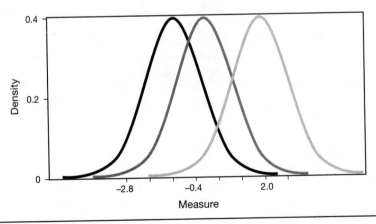

Figure 3.6 The concept of reproducibility.

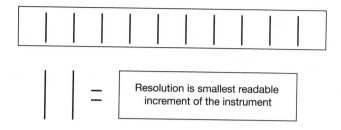

Figure 3.7 The concept of resolution.

MSA Aspects of the Acceptance Sampling Proposal

The sensor for the acceptance sampling plan proposal is a human interpreting the results of a specific physical test, the melting point test. Clearly there are potential operator effects to consider and also device-related uncertainty due to the inherent repeatability of the test method and equipment. It would be quite appropriate to perform a MSA of this procedure. Because the melting test is a destructive test, however, it does not allow one to perform exact repeats. One option is to select product produced under homogeneous conditions and use these as pseudo-repeats. There will certainly be a confusion of pure repeatability and reproducibility (R&R) with some product changes, but it will often yield a workable answer. Table 3.2 shows the possible results of running this MSA on the acceptance sampling plan system. Notice that the performance, gage R&R greater than 30%, is deemed unacceptable in most circumstances. And a large measurement error can have drastic impact on the guarantee of the acceptance sampling plan.

MSA Aspects of the Fail-Safe Proposal

In the case of the fail-safe system, the sensor is fully automatic with a sensor that fluoresces the still semi-molten plastic and measures the result with a visual detector. It applies some postprocessing to determine the validity of the sample and then adds this to a database. A Kalman filter is applied to this database and an automatic feedback adjustment can be made to the process to return the process to conformity. The system also marks the bags that measured out of specification and the system automatically sends these to a reclamation process. Figure 3.8 shows a diagram of this process.

Table 3.2 Measurement systems analysis for acceptance sampling.

Source	Components	6 × components	Percent tolerance
Operator	1.1 mpu	6.6 mpu	66%
Equipment/test	0.5 mpu	3.0 mpu	30%
R&R	1.21 mpu	7.21 mpu	72.1%

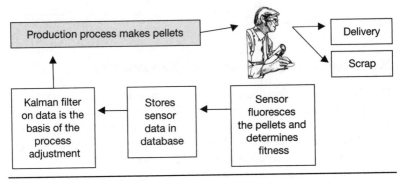

Figure 3.8 The fail-safe adjustment process.

Although this system is not foolproof, it is considered a fail-safe because there is no human decision-making going on as a final check on the product disposition. The behavior of this system, from a measurement systems standpoint, depends on the functioning of the sensor, on the postprocessing activity, and on the Kalman filter performance. The marking system and the automatic routing method are the actions that it provides. In this example operators play little role so reproducibility is unlikely to be important. Now there are additional impacts that the standard MSA ignores that must be evaluated, including: data collection errors, data storage errors, postprocessing computation errors, and uncertainty embedded in the performance of the Kalman filter algorithm. Table 3.3 illustrates a possible partial uncertainty analysis for the fail-safe proposal.

Total uncertainty combines the partial uncertainties in a root mean square computation:

Total uncertainty = sqrt (sum of squared components) = 0.0521

An uncertainty interval is then constructed as +/− 2 times the total uncertainty.

Uncertainty interval = +/− 2 × 0.0521 = 0.1142 mpu

Table 3.3 Partial uncertainty analysis of fail-safe.

Component name	Components	Type
Power supply	0.004 mpu	External
Lamp filament	0.012 mpu	External
Lens cleanliness	0.034 mpu	Test
Calibration	0.002 mpu	Test
Data transfer	0.029 mpu	Test
Data storage	0.005 mpu	Expertise
Algorithm details	0.023 mpu	Expertise

MSA Aspects of the Auto-Quality Program

The auto-quality program appears to be completely a human-mediated visual inspection of the product. Essentially, it is trying to accomplish something similar to the fail-safe system, but by using color as perceived by the human eye. A sample is taken and the perceived color is compared by the operator to a set of prepared standards displayed as pictures on a chart. The operator then decides based on this comparison to adjust the process settings to re-center the process. The sample is specified to be a certain size and shape, and the location is specified. If the perceived color is too extreme, then the material is removed manually from the system by the operator. Figure 3.9 shows the flow of this system.

From a measurement systems standpoint, the systems will likely have a large reproducibility effect since it depends so heavily on the operator. Other areas of concern are the conditions behind the visual inspection. Perhaps there is a specially-designed light that can become dirty and hence affect the judgment results. There are also many sample preparation or collection effects caused by variations in the sample parameters such as size and shape. There is also an effect of the resolution of the standards chart. If there are only two or three choices, then this could impact error to a great extent. Table 3.4 shows the possible results of an attribute MSA for this system.

Since the inspection measurement is the engine that drives the inspection quality management system, it is critical to have adequate performance on this end to achieve good overall performance. However, the performance of the overall system will almost always be better than that to be expected from knowledge of the individual components themselves. This is due to the statistical and mathematical treatment of the raw data coming from the sensors. This is the main reason that integration of simple inspection systems into a whole can produce dramatically better results. A good integrated system should outperform an unorganized set

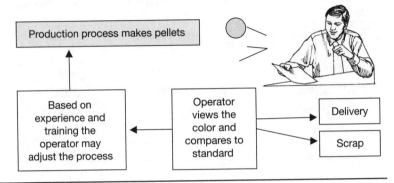

Figure 3.9 The diagram of the auto-quality process.

Table 3.4 Measurement systems analysis for auto-quality proposal.

Operator	Effectiveness	Effectiveness to reference	False alarm	Miss rate
Emmanuel	82%	82%	10%	0%
LaTasha	93%	90%	6%	2%
Benjamin	90%	90%	4%	6%

of simple systems in statistical quality performance, cost, reliability, and efficiency. A complete discussion of this integration process must wait until Chapter 10, after a discussion is given of these three basic subsystems of modern inspection quality management.

Chapter 3 Value Propositions

1. Sensors can provide a variety of inputs to inspection measurements.

2. Inspection measurements can have powerful image enhancement.

3. Uncertainty analysis can be applied to inspections measurements.

4. Inspection measurements must have good repeatability, reproducibility, and resolution.

4

Acceptance Sampling Principles

INTRODUCTION TO SAMPLING

Sampling (Cochran 1963) is the selection of certain possible inspections from the set of all possible inspections on a process. The manufacturing process is assumed to be running more or less continuously compared to the frequency of sample selection. The quality technician or engineer can use a sensor-based measurement system to interact with this manufacturing process and provide an inspection. The number of these possible measurements is finite and forces one to turn the continuous process dynamics into a sequence of snapshots or frames at discrete times. Even in the rare cases where the process is monitored continuously, the treatment of the inspection is usually broken down for practical purposes.

The sampling plan is the specification of the locations and times of inspection and these choices can have a tremendous influence on performance of the inspection system. When there are multiple sensors, of identical or dissimilar types, the sampling plan can also control the pattern of allocation of the samples across the individual sensors. The number of samples refers to the total number of measurements that are to be taken. Both aspects of sampling, number and type of samples, can affect the cost of implementing the inspection plan.

AN AUDIT CASE STUDY

A government inspector needs to audit a facility warehouse in order to assess the tax rate correctly. Specifically, the tax rate depends on the class of the product contained in the warehouse because this class ultimately relates to market value of the product. The time that the product spends stored in the warehouse is related to depreciation and thus also affects the tax rate. Unfortunately, there is no automation installed in this particular warehouse so there is no way to track individual product codes, but the different product classes are stored in distinct parts of the warehouse.

A suitable sampling plan might be to select completely random samples from each of the distinct parts of the warehouse. This should ensure that all product types are inspected in a fair way. Within each product type there must be adequate samples to estimate the number of items at time t and then again at least one other time $t + 1$ so that a rate of retention can be estimated. It is decided to sample 4% of the storage racks at random and do counts of products. These counts will then be extrapolated to the total number of available racks and positions. This procedure will be applied each week for a prescribed period of time. This plan is shown in Figure 4.1.

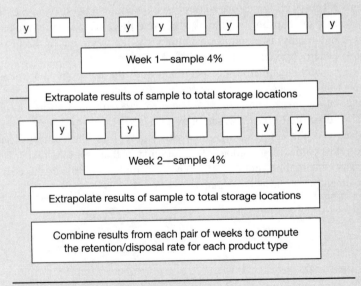

Figure 4.1 The audit sampling plan.

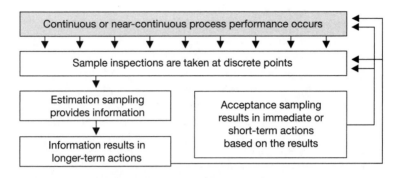

Figure 4.2 Indirect and direct sampling modes.

The ultimate objective of any sampling plan is to produce useful information about the process. But there are at least two actions that this information can promulgate. In indirect application the data are usually processed, often by a human being, and are used as part of a decision to change the process or to alter some activity. Often this kind of sampling produces an estimate of some process characteristic, and further action is delayed and only partially based on this measurement. A direct action is when there is minimal processing and the actions to be taken are more or less automatic or algorithmic, based on the measurement. Often this direct approach does not need to have a human decision in the loop. Real inspection systems can fall along a continuum between direct and indirect. See Figure 4.2 for the sampling options.

ACCEPTANCE SAMPLING CONCEPTS

Acceptance sampling (Schilling 1982) is a direct action form of sampling. Although there are many variations that have been introduced over the nearly 80 years of application in the area, most acceptance sampling plans specify actions algorithmically based on the results, and they have two possible actions: take more samples and rectify the nonconforms. The best way in which to demonstrate this is through a simple example.

THE LAUGHING PUMPKIN FINAL TEST CASE STUDY

A company that specializes in Halloween electronics needs to maintain, at most, 5% nonconform rates on its popular laughing pumpkin item. This is a molded foam pumpkin that plays a re-corded laugh track in response to a nearby loud sound. A large chain of novelty stores has agreed to stock these items if the quality guarantee can be met. Everything needs to be put into place for the shipment two weeks from today.

An acceptance sampling plan is implemented in which each shipment of 30 pumpkins is treated as a batch. An inspector, a regular employee on light duty, is assigned to test a random selection of 4 pumpkins from each batch. The test method is defined and the inspector trained. If 1 or more of the 4 pumpkins fails to activate under the test conditions, then the entire set of 30, or whatever remains to be tested, is set aside for exhaustive testing. A shipment of 30 is then constructed from as many batches as necessary to get 30 correctly performing pumpkins. If none of the 4 from a batch fail the test, then the whole batch is sent to the shipping department as is. This plan was chosen because the textbooks state that this guarantees a 4% average outgoing quality limit, which meets the needs of the company for a 5% level.

This simpleminded inspection approach results in direct improvement of the outgoing or delivered quality of the process by its rectification action. It selectively changes the number of samples adaptively based on its estimate of the process noncon-form rate. It specifies only two sampling plans: randomly or 100%. And yet, this approach provides a robust, effective way in which to give a statistical guarantee on the outgoing quality. Consider Figure 4.3 for an illustration of this simple plan.

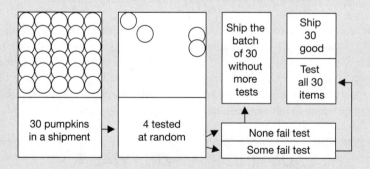

Figure 4.3 The pumpkin testing acceptance sampling plan.

Performance of Acceptance Sampling Plans

The statistical quality performance of this simple plan is easy to derive. Consider the pathway shown in Figure 4.3 to understand this. Within a particular batch there are a number of nonconforms sprinkled in some unknown way. The acceptance sampling plan specifies that a random sample, 18 in the case of the plastic pellet example, be selected from the batch of 1000 bags. One of the 18 samples bags is opened and a handful of pellets is removed and tested. If this first bag passes the test then the procedure is repeated for a second bag and so on. If any bag fails the melting test, then the entire batch of 1000 bags is sent for further inspection, and each bag is tested for conformance to specifications. Rectification occurs when any tested, failed bag is replaced by a conforming bag. Thus there are always 1000 bags sent to the customer.

The chance that a sampled bag contains a nonconforming pellet depends on the number of nonconforms in the whole batch. The probability that the sample, only 18 of a possible 1000 after all, will contain at least one of these nonconforming bags depends in turn on this more basic probability. Statisticians have computed this probability for any possible number of beginning nonconforms and this relationship is shown in Figure 4.4.

This plan will perform in this manner as long as the probability of nonconforms stays consistent and as long as the sample is random with respect to the hidden pattern. The curve shown in Figure 4.4 is really the heart of the statistical quality performance of the plan, but it is often more convenient to display it in a more appealing fashion. To do this, consider the impact on the outgoing quality of a particular batch of bags. If no nonconforms are found

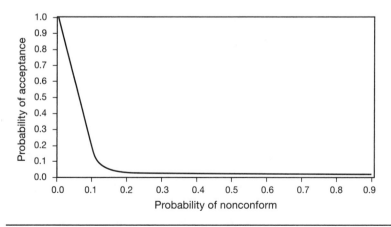

Figure 4.4 The probability of acceptance relationship.

in the samples, then the method specifies that we replace the sampled bags by good ones and send the whole lot without further testing. A moment's thought will convince you that the unchecked samples will likely have just as many nonconforms as they did before this sampling process. There is no improvement and you get what you started with. On the other hand, if a sample is rejected, then the whole 1000 bags are eventually replaced with good ones before delivery. So the quality of these rejected lots is perfect with zero nonconforms. The average delivered quality is a function of the number of nonconforms to begin with and the sampling plan can be displayed as in Figure 4.5.

It is a pleasant feature of these kinds of curves that they will have a single maximum value called the average outgoing quality limit (AOQL). Users tend to focus on this feature as a simple specification of the statistical quality performance of the acceptance sampling plan. It is important to note that there are other features that might be important as well, such as the variance of the outgoing quality level, but these will not be discussed further here.

Cost of the Acceptance Sampling Plan

Most of the components of the cost of implementing the acceptance sampling plan are related to the specific costs associated with the system. In the pellet example these include costs of installing the equipment and training the inspectors. There are two costs that are directly related to the sampling plan that is applied. Specifically, there is a fixed cost of $18 per batch of 1000 because it is required to take the 18 samples.

There is a variable cost related to the plan as well because of the 100% cleansing that is required when nonconforming samples are found. A little

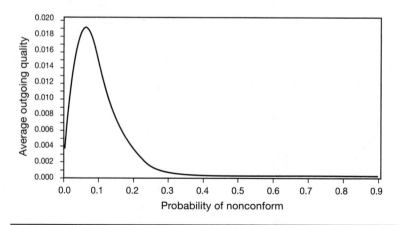

Figure 4.5 The outgoing quality relationship.

thought will show that the cost is at least $1000 per batch if it is rejected in the sampling. This is averaged with the cost of $18 for an accepted batch. So the average cost directly caused by the plan is dependent on the production nonconform rate and can be displayed as in Figure 4.6.

Reliability of the Acceptance Sampling Plan

The reliability of the plan has been discussed in some detail where it was shown that there were issues with the test equipment reliability and the operator dependability. Most of these issues are independent of the sampling plan itself. But one aspect should probably be dealt with in more detail; the number of expected failures of the entire inspection/cleansing system. The reliability of an individual test was given as 80% for a month. This means that there is a 20% chance that an individual tester will fail within a month. But this month probably should be re-expressed as service time, rather than calendar time. If a month means a month of normal sampling usage, that is, 18 tests per batch, then this means that it is 20% probable that a device will fail if it performs 18 tests per shift times 2 shifts times 30 days per month to equal 1080 tests. The number of tests could be higher if the same equipment is used for the cleansing activities, perhaps on the off-shift. The curve shown in Figure 4.7 shows the average number of extra tests to be done per batch dependent on the incoming quality level.

There are other aspects to do with the administration of reliability resources that are important as well, such as: spare parts, preventive maintenance, predictive maintenance, repair time, and staffing that must be considered for any system. Most of these are affected by the sampling plan, but the details will not be completely developed in this example. Keep in

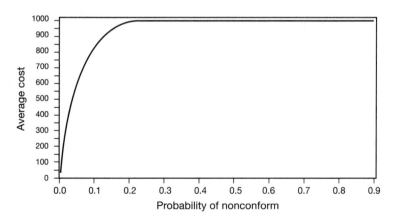

Figure 4.6 The variable portion of the cost of the plan.

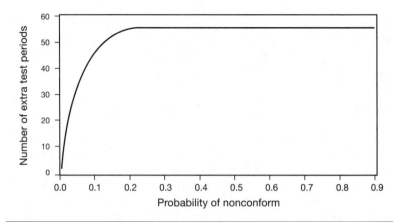

Figure 4.7 The reliability of the sampling plan.

mind that reliability is often best thought as quality through time (Lawless 1983) and so is important to ensure reliability for any inspection system before the product is delivered to the customer.

Efficiency of the Acceptance Sampling Plan

The efficiency of the acceptance sampling plan was discussed in part in Chapter 2, but certain aspects that depend directly on the sampling plan will be discussed in more detail in this section. Efficiency is the time spent in critical or value-added activity compared to the total time to finish the task. When the normal sampling is being performed, the 18 samples must be collected randomly. The process could select these to deliver them to the inspector or the inspector could do the selection manually, which could mean a huge difference in time to complete the task.

When samples fail, the questionable bags are shunted away from the delivery path to an intensive 100% cleansing pathway. This might very well utilize the same inspection posts on the off-shift and thus would involve other personnel. These personnel might not be as well-trained as the original inspectors or they may employ a different method. Thus the time spent on cleansing samples could be more per bag than the inspection sample, say 2 minutes rather than 1 minute. In this case, the efficiency of the whole acceptance sampling plan system will drag, and the amount of drag will depend on the number of nonconforms that are created by the production process and then delivered to the inspection posts. Figure 4.8 shows the efficiency versus the incoming nonconform rate.

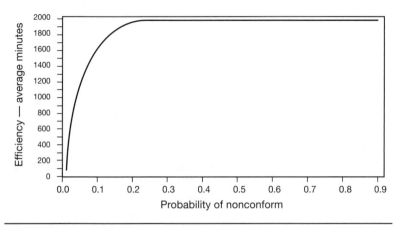

Figure 4.8 The efficiency of the sampling plan.

SUMMARY OF PROPERTIES OF ACCEPTANCE SAMPLING PLANS

The four features that are demonstrated for the example proposals can be replicated for any acceptance sampling plan that might be devised. Table 4.1 is a summary of the various types of acceptance sampling plans in terms of operational flow.

Many acceptance sampling plans do not adhere strictly to the rules of operation of the standard textbook plans. Therefore the various characteristics as given in Table 4.1 may not be exactly correct. If plans like these are applied in ways that are specific to a process, then usually simulation (Murray-Smith 1995) must be applied to fully understand the various performance traits. A simulation model is a set of code that mimics the important features of the physical system. It has at least three advantages over studying the real process: it is usually much faster, cheaper, and more modifiable. However, the results of the simulation model are merely one instance of the process and are only as good as the model.

EXAMPLE OF MODIFIED SAMPLING PLAN

If there is one nonconform in the sample of 18, then an additional sample of 10 on either side of the found nonconform is taken. If no further nonconforms are found, then the batch is accepted. If an additional nonconform is found, then the batch is rejected. But the cleansing is done by taking sub-samples of 100 consecutive bags. If there are no nonconforms in the 100, then no further cleansing is done. If nonconforms are found, then progressive sets of 100 are continued. See Figure 4.9.

Table 4.1 A summary of acceptance sampling plan types.

Type of Sampling Plan	Description of the Flow of the Sampling Plan
Single-level batch attribute	Choose batch—1 sample—attribute—attribute—100% or sampling
Double-level batch attribute	Choose batch—take 2 samples—attribute—100% or sampling
Batch-attribute scheme	Choose batch—take 1 sample—attribute—1 of 3 intensities
Continuous attribute	Clearance interval—sample—attribute—switch between the 2
Batch-variable plan	Choose batch—1 sample—variable—100% or sampling
Continuous variable	Clearance interval—sample—variable—switch between the 2

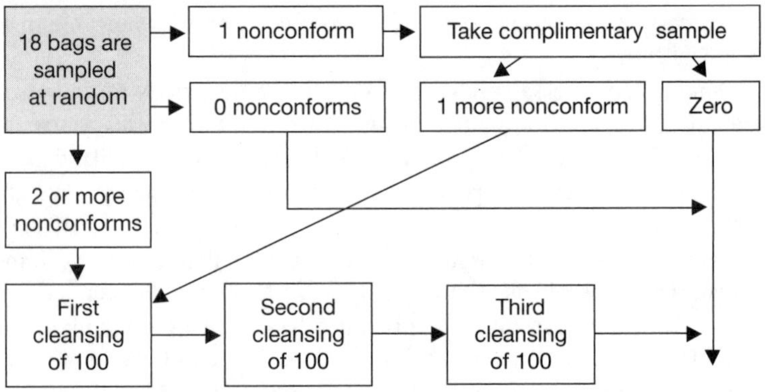

Figure 4.9 The modified acceptance sampling plan.

Chapter 4 Value Propositions

1. Acceptance sampling works through control of further inspection system itself.

2. There is a wide variety of plans that fit any need.

3. Average outgoing quality curves demonstrate performance of the plan.

4. Average fraction inspected curves can be used to evaluate cost.

5. Practical plans almost always require modification.

5

Product and Process Control Plans

A second major branch of actions that can be driven by the inspection quality management system is the control plan (Lieberman 1965). This type of activity is distinguished from that of the adjustment activity that is discussed in the next chapter by the fact that it initiates actions only upon the passing of a threshold (Box 1974). For most readers, the image that should come to mind is that of a standard process control chart like the Shewhart chart. But there is no reason why such a chart must be restricted to process control only. Under the umbrella of continuous improvement, one can control the product as well as the process. On the simplest such control chart, action is taken only when an observed point exceeds the control limits. Usually these actions are not simple adjustments of the process, but are often more severe dislocations. For example, such an action might be to call in maintenance and completely reset the machine. Or it might be a symptom that a new supplier of copy paper has been introduced and the quality is distinctly different from the original source. In the adjustment approach described in the next chapter, the changes to the process are less severe. Figure 5.1 demonstrates the control approach.

STATISTICAL CONTROL APPROACH

Statistics (Grant 1996) is a science and a methodology for making decisions under uncertainty. Typically, this uncertainty is modeled as an additive error term that is present in each individual measurement. Because these measurement errors can add or subtract from the true value, in other words, cause a false positive or a false negative mistake, most practical statistical

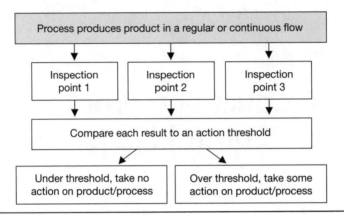

Figure 5.1 Process flow of the control approach.

methods involve a decision or action threshold. That is, on one side of the threshold the decision-maker makes one kind of decision, while on the other side, an entirely different one. Depending on the conditions of application this threshold can be formulated as a confidence interval, as a critical test value, or as a control limit. Regardless of the way in which it is represented, the defining characteristic is the existence of a threshold that cleanly separates one type of decision from another. See Figure 5.2 for a graphical depiction of the threshold approach.

In a process application, the limits are called *control limits* and commonly appear as two parallel lines on either side of a center or target line. These lines are placed so that points falling outside the limits justify a conclusion that the process mean has shifted off-target and that follow-up actions should be initiated in order to re-center it. Points falling within the interior region between the lines lead to the conclusion that the process has not shifted significantly off-target and no immediate action is recommended. This approach of comparing datapoints to a preestablished threshold is the method that is termed *statistical control* and is shown in Figure 5.3.

APPLICATION TO PRODUCT CONTROL

The engine that drives the statistical control method is an inspection. Usually this is a measurement made on a product output from the process at specific sample points spaced regularly in time. If the individual measurement points are plotted on the chart for comparison with the thresholds, then the chart is known as an *individuals chart*. More commonly the plot is of the average of several clustered points or their range on what are termed

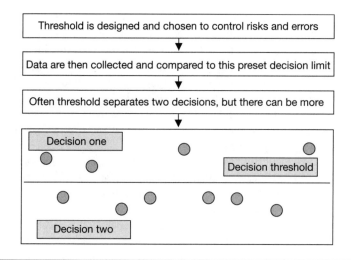

Figure 5.2 The decision threshold approach.

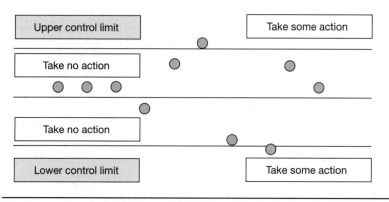

Figure 5.3 A standard control chart.

x-bar charts and *range charts*, respectively. The effect of the averaging is to enhance the power of the charts to detect shifts and hence is a method of postprocessing the inspection data to make them more effective. Generally speaking, the averaging does require more process time to elapse before new points are available for plotting, so there is a trade-off of reaction time for better support for the decisions that are made.

The basic measurement is often quite similar for the control method regardless of whether the field of application is that of process or product control. And when the chart is an individuals chart (Duncan 1974), even the plotted points are indistinguishable for each type of inspection application. It is the interpretation of the chart that is afforded by the postprocessing of the measurements that is the distinguishing feature. And this interpretation drives the specific actions that are initiated as a result of the inspection. It is these actions, as mentioned previously, that are critical to determining the type of control. If the action is a re-centering of the process, then the inspection is driving process control. If the action that is mandated is a simple retest or re-measurement of the part, then the application is most likely to be one of product control. If the action is a change in the frequency of sampling or location of samples, then again it is product control. If the action is a product disposition by sending the item to the scrap heap, then again product control is the target. On the other hand, if the action is to halt the production process and take remedial action, then it is inspection control of process. Each of these different actions of process and product control will be dealt with separately in the following sections.

Considering the case of the auto-quality program proposal for the plastic pellet manufacturer, the operator could apply a threshold control plan simultaneously for product and process modification. In this case the threshold is probably not a standard control chart, but operates instead as a comparison of the sampled product to a prescribed chart of possible aspects. This comparison depends on all the postprocessing that is implied by the fact that it is mediated by a human being. Once the determination of color is accomplished, the result must be matched to the standard to which it corresponds. Thus, there are multiple thresholds that are part of the inspection procedure. One of these thresholds controls the disposition of the product itself. If the measurement falls over the conformance threshold, the operator sends it into the scrap circuit. Otherwise it is accepted as conforming and routed to the next work post. This is direct control of the product quality through inspection.

In addition to the product disposition activity, the inspection of color also is used by the operator to determine a process control action. In this case all of the thresholds are active. Depending on which standard the inspected product most closely matches, there is a recommended modification to the process. Perhaps this recommended action can be modified according to the experience of the operator as well. For the vast majority of applications, the process and product thresholds are probably different. In any case, some kind of threshold determines the action that the operator takes. This corrective action could be as simple as "hit reset" when over the limits. Or it could stimulate a call to maintenance for follow-up action. Or it could require further checks and retests and the application of specific algorithms to set the corrective action.

INTERPRETATION OF THE THRESHOLD APPROACH

To establish the appropriate threshold, it is imperative to understand what the action is intended to accomplish. For process control, the inspection is usually interpreted or modeled as a constant mean positioned to hit a target that is contaminated by random variation due to a combination of normal process variation and normal measurement error. If this interpretation is true, then it is straightforward to calculate the probability that a measurement point will fall within the threshold limits. Likewise, it is possible to compute that when an observed point falls outside the limit, then the probability is low that the process is on target. So it makes sense to assume that the process has shifted and that follow-up actions should be taken. For example, it is common for process control purposes to choose the threshold limits so that the probability of a false alarm is a 0.3%. This ensures that signals will only be given when the mean has changed dramatically!

For product control, the interpretation of the identical data is different. Now the observed value is thought to be a true value of the product masked by whatever measurement error there might be. The measurement value is an indication of the true value, but is raised or lowered arbitrarily by the act of measurement. The postprocessing for inspection purposes sets different thresholds that are based on this model and that allow for this measurement error. That is, the limits for product disposition are widened so that they allow for this unavoidable error. The purpose is to ensure that there is a high probability that the true measurement is outside (or inside) the threshold. Thus the limits should be set based on measurement error, rather than the total variation of process and measurement error. And these limits are centered around a product tolerance rather than the target. For example, one could start with the true upper tolerance limit and then adjust it to allow for measurement error. Backing down two standard deviations of measurement error will give roughly 95% certainty that the real value is less than the threshold. See Figure 5.4 to see how this might work.

There are some situations in which the two thresholds, the ones for product and process control, will be identical, but this is likely to be extremely rare. If the measurement system guidelines are respected and the measurement system variability is less than 30% of the total variation, then the relative positions of the two thresholds are as shown in Figure 5.5.

Note that this relationship is easiest to see on an individuals chart, but it is certainly possible to run both process and product decisions off averages of several values. The only adjustment for the process control threshold is to account for the reduction in variability due to the averaging,

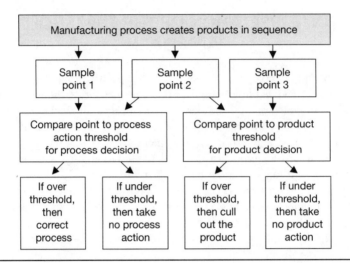

Figure 5.4 The logic of the auto-quality inspections.

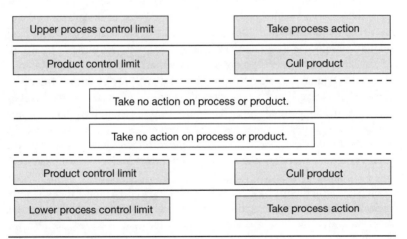

Figure 5.5 The product and process threshold charts.

namely a shrinking of the limits. For the product control, the action is not so obvious. Perhaps four repeat measurements are made on each bag and disposition can fairly be done on an average of the four repeat measurements. Then the measurement error can be shrunk independently and the product control threshold will become narrower. Figure 5.6 illustrates the relationship between the individuals and the average charts.

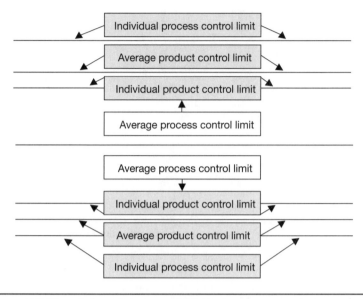

Figure 5.6 The relationship between individual and average charts.

STATISTICAL QUALITY PERFORMANCE OF THE THRESHOLD CONTROL PLAN

The statistical quality performance of an inspection control plan is determined by the specific probabilities that are chosen for the various thresholds. By convention, process control limits are set at 99.7%, which equates to a 0.3% of a false negative and a false positive that varies as the graph in Figure 5.7 shows. Product control limits are often set at 95% so that the chance of a false positive is less than 5% and the chance of false negative is around 95%. The actual number of errors that are made will depend on these probabilities applied to the number of item that are produced per time unit.

COST OF THE THRESHOLD CONTROL PLAN

Some of the costs that were described earlier, such as setup, training, and payroll issues, do not depend directly on the parameters of the threshold control plan that is used. But there are some costs that will depend on the type and features of the threshold plan that is used. For example, if there is a productivity loss that results from the spreading of operator attention

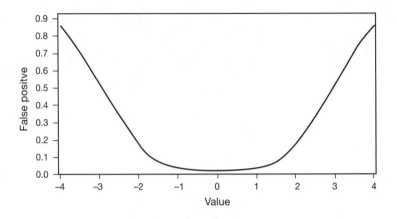

Figure 5.7 The false positive error for the process control chart.

between operations and inspection control of 1%, then this could worsen if more than the anticipated number of nonconforms is given. Each time a product is dispositioned to the scrap circuit, it will conceivably require some additional outlay of resources. If the standard send-to-scrap circuit action costs $10 per event, then the actual loss will depend on the number of times that a disposition is required. This disposition in turn is determined by the number of times that the product control limits are exceeded. For a good process this might be only 5% of the time, if the limits are chosen as usual at 95% on individual values, but could increase drastically if the process is not running well. This function of cost versus false alarms can be displayed in a graph, as in Figure 5.8.

RELIABILITY OF THE THRESHOLD CONTROL PLAN

Reliability of the control plan depends on the equipment reliability and operator dependability, as described earlier. It can be affected by the inspection control plan itself in at least three ways. First, the worse the production process, the more times the test will reject the sample. This is likely to affect both the operator and the equipment reliability. The effectiveness and willingness of the operator to conduct the test properly will often be compromised when a good proportion of time is spent in dispositioning product and adjusting the process. It might also be possible that a preventive maintenance plan is triggered by the number of signals that are seen, with

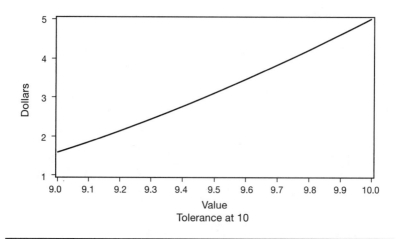

Figure 5.8 The process control cost as a function of true product value.

the assumption that it may be the device rather than the process that is misleading. If this is true then the more signals that are given the sooner this preventive maintenance will happen. This may actually result in better reliability since the device is presumably recalibrated more often than would occur normally. Figure 5.9 shows what could happen to reliability of the system if the operator dependability detonates with too frequent signals.

EFFICIENCY OF THE THRESHOLD CONTROL PLAN

Efficiency of the control plan has components that are unaffected by the control plan itself as well as components that are affected. The process time that is required to take a sample is specified by protocol and so cannot be accelerated without consequences. But the inspection time to prepare the sample, to make the inspection, and to do the comparison are prime candidates for improvements in efficiency. It is possible that this efficiency would drop if the operator became saturated with too many signals, but this is not likely to be severe until complete saturation occurs. So it is likely that the efficiency of this control plan is fixed by the design of the procedure to a great extent and is relatively insensitive to the performance of the plan itself.

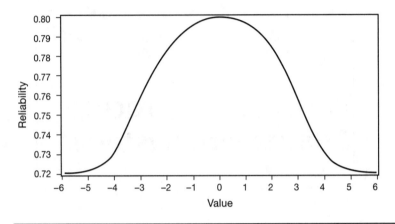

Figure 5.9 Operator reliability as a function of process average.

Chapter 5 Value Propositions

1. Inspection control plans have decision thresholds.

2. Control charts can guide process or product intervention.

3. Inspection controls are intermediate in receiving inputs and in establishing actions.

4. Both individuals and summary charts are valuable.

6

Product and Process Adjustment Systems

CHARACTERISTICS OF ADJUSTMENT SYSTEMS

The in-line inspection fail-safe scheme that has appeared in previous discussions is a product and process adjustment scheme. Just as there are various modifications and adaptations that can be instituted in acceptance sampling and control schemes, there are many versions of adjustment schemes. In general, an adjustment scheme can be characterized by the following three features:

1. It measures nearly every discrete part.

2. It makes some adjustment on every inspection.

3. It can take rapid action.

The distinctions between adjustment and control plans can be subtle in some cases, but in most real situations it is easy to tell to which category they belong. The example given by the fail-safe can be instructive in this way. When the fail-safe is active, a measurement is made on every bag of pellets. This information is postprocessed through an algorithm like the Kalman filter (Downing 1980) to provide an immediate feedback control action that is intended to be applied to the very next bag of production. But the same information can also be manipulated or postprocessed through the appropriate inspection system to automatically classify the current bag as conforming or nonconforming and start a sequence of product adjustment actions. That is, the adjustment can be the basis of a process or a product inspection scheme.

The Kalman filter is a mathematical procedure by which one can smooth and predict measurement values for state space-based model of a process through time. It presupposes that two types of relationships exist in the process. First, there is a transition equation that describes the manner in which the state of the process progresses from one measurement to the next. This is assumed to be linear and is expressed as transition matrix. This must be fitted to the process data. The other equation is the measurement equation, which links the state variable to the measurement quantities including any measurement noise that may be induced. This also is linear and expressed as a matrix that must be fitted to the data. Because these equations take account of the measurement process explicitly, it is possible to use the fitted Kalman filter model to strip away the measurement noise to produce filtered values at the current time or any time into the future. And since the measurement equation fits a model of the measurement effects, it can also be used to describe these effects for product classification.

Consider the method by which one would utilize the in-line adjustment system to guide product disposition in this inspection-based fail-safe procedure. The problem is, as it was in the control plan, to make a good decision in the face of possible measurement error. The Kalman filter, similarly to other adjustment models, utilizes a sequence of measurements to estimate the true value of the quantity at any particular moment in time. In order to do this, the model not only includes a process dynamics component, but also a measurement model complete with an estimate of measurement error. The complete model can cope with various patterns and trends in time along with this measurement error. One can use this model of the process to filter the current observation of its measurement error and can then use limits similar to the control plan limits to give a confidence that the true value is really outside of produce tolerances. Or one can use the model to predict the next observation and then check to see if the newly collected measurement falls within error bounds of this prediction. Either way, one can adjust the probabilities to get a set of thresholds to guide product sorting and disposition. Because of the dependence of this approach on current and previous measurements, it is again an example of postprocessing of the basic measurements so they provide a much more powerful inspection on which to guide actions. Figure 6.1 illustrates this procedure.

For process adjustment, the Kalman filter approach and related adjustment approaches use the identical model for a different purpose and perhaps with a completely different mechanism involved in obtaining the required result. Now, instead of simply estimating the current value with measurement error filtered out, or making a prediction of the next observation, the model is used in a process adjustment approach. Specifically, the algorithm computes a suggested adjustment to the process to correct the

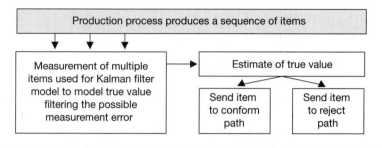

Figure 6.1 The product disposition decision in adjustment.

process automatically. Note that this requires a different set of assumptions than did the control approach. Whereas the control model assumes that process upsets needed to be handled outside the process, the adjustment methodology uses leverage points that are already contained in the system. For example, the correction may be temperature change in the extruder or a pressure change. Or it may be a change in process takeaway speed that is intended to move the process center nearer to the target. This approach treats variation as something that can be corrected or adjusted within the system, rather than by large-scale changes forced onto the system as a whole.

The proposed adjustment action is formulated in such a way as to exactly cancel the expected or predicted departure from the target. Note that it cannot anticipate the actual measurement error since this is assumed to be independent, but it can allow for possible errors. The Kalman filter or other methods are simply models. And as models they are not perfect, so the approach constantly updates and refines the model. It is the inspection of each item and the adjustment of the process at every sampling point that makes this an adjustment process. There is no threshold involved. The predicted or filtered value is treated as if it were the true value of the item and subsequent actions follow from this conclusion. Such an inspection adjustment process can also be operated on a sampling basis but usually the performance of the plan increases with faster inspections. But no matter if the sampling pattern and frequency begins to resemble a control plan, a critical difference is that adjustment plans do not typically have thresholds. They act on every available measurement without regard to its position relative to limits. Figure 6.2 shows the decision logic of the adjustment process.

The process and product adjustment models such as the Kalman filter automatically update themselves in response to inputs from the inspections that are made. Thus there will usually be a time lag to collect enough new inspections to change the current model. This makes good sense for any slowly changing system since the current model is a combination of old and

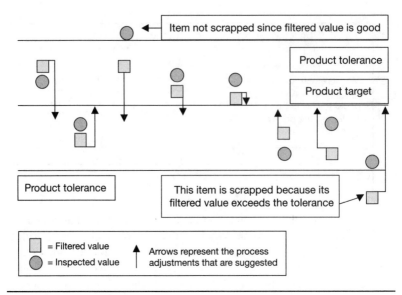

Figure 6.2 The decision logic of the adjustment process.

new data, but it can cause a slower response to rapid or sudden shifts in the process. Since the control actions for product and process are formulated from this model, it is generally not possible to make dramatic changes to the entire system as is possible with process control. Figure 6.3 shows how this might work correctly while Figure 6.4 shows some possible problems.

STATISTICAL PERFORMANCE FOR THE ADJUSTMENT PLAN

The in-line inspection or fail-safe system proposed for the pellet company has an unusual statistical guarantee in that it promises 100% ability to stop certain deviations from target. Statistically, one does not usually encounter such strong guarantees. More likely, the chance of an error in classification depends on how far the true product value is from the tolerance value. The system does have a 2% error in overprotection that will result in the erroneous rejection of product that is really conforming. Since leaks or false positives result in the mistaken delivery of nonconforming product to a customer, they are usually more penalizing than false alarms. So this system seems to make the right kind of trade-off between the two kinds of errors. If one wanted to check this manufacturer's promise, it would be necessary to either run a test on the whole system or try to validate each step of the

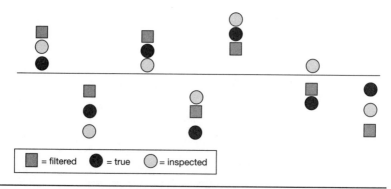

Figure 6.3 Example of good Kalman adjustment. The filter values match the true values so adjustment will be good.

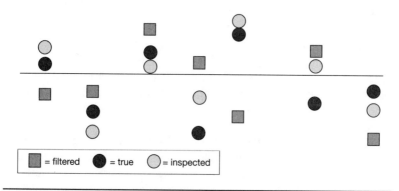

Figure 6.4 Example of poor Kalman adjustment. The filtered values miss the true values so adjustment will be poor.

process and build up the overall guarantee from these components. Unless the process changes and invalidates the guarantee, there is not much more to say about the protection of this device.

COST FOR THE ADJUSTMENT PLAN

Since the cost is fixed for this plan, it does not really depend on the particular plan performance. Perhaps if the system finds more nonconforms than was designed it may become more costly, but this is not clear. The variable cost portion of the cost that is related to this system is driven by the manufacturing process performance. The more nonconforms that are created the more that will be rejected, and hence the cost will rise as shown in Figure 6.5.

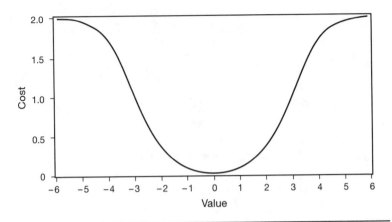

Figure 6.5 The variable cost in the fail-safe system.

The fixed costs associated with the fail-safe system are the largest ones. There is the purchase and installation cost of $1 million and the ongoing preventative maintenance as well. But there is another fixed cost due to the slowdown of the manufacturing process to operate the fail-safe adjustment device. This is stated to be a 3% loss of cycle time, so it could be quite substantial over long production runs. This cycle time loss could also be potentially influenced by the number of rejected products if the manufacturing process is poor. Since the cycle includes the identification, marking, and diversion of failed products, it seems reasonable that the cycle time impact would be greater when the manufacturing process is off-target or erratic. If we assume that the nominal 3% loss is when the process is centered, then when it is off-center it should lead to increased losses, as illustrated in Figure 6.6.

RELIABILITY OF THE ADJUSTMENT PLAN

The reliability of the in-line inspection device is seemingly assured if the maintenance requirements are met. But there are many components to the system, such as the computer algorithm and the database, that may have to be changed when new versions of operating systems are launched or new security protocols are adapted. There is also a good chance that the system will perform as guaranteed if all conditions of the contract are satisfied, but performance will fall off with age or excess usage or delayed maintenance.

For example, it might be possible to get from the vendor a plot of reliability versus the length of the interval between preventive maintenance

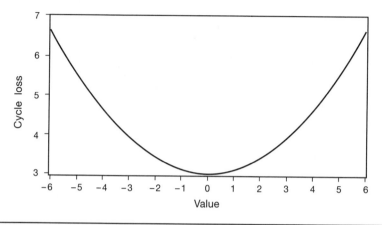

Figure 6.6 Cycle time losses with respect to process performance.

events founded on their experience with similar devices. In this case, the unit seems to be relatively unique and a bit experimental, so the curve may more likely be based on engineering knowledge and laboratory tests. Such a plot could show that the six-month recommended maintenance interval is not necessary in the first five years, but after nine years even more frequent interventions are necessary to meet requirements. Such a reliability versus interval and age could appear as in Figure 6.7.

EFFICIENCY OF THE ADJUSTMENT PLAN

The efficiency of the in-line inspection system is totally unspecified in the current description. There is a near certain loss of productivity, but it is unclear just how much this might increase if the system is faced with an overload of too many nonconforms. This was shown to result in rising costs, but could also result in lost time. Additionally, the Kalman filter and software might be fooled if too many nonconforms in a row are generated. They might interpret such events as a more fundamental change in the system's dynamics, which may result in models that incorporate them. Once the system has entered one of these abnormal periods, it may take some time for the model to correct itself after the system finally rights itself. These systems might also need sufficient start-up time to reach full efficiency and may need to be tuned for each product code. The stated production losses of 3% might be correct for stable running conditions, but may end up being a lot worse for start-ups, shutdowns, or system upsets.

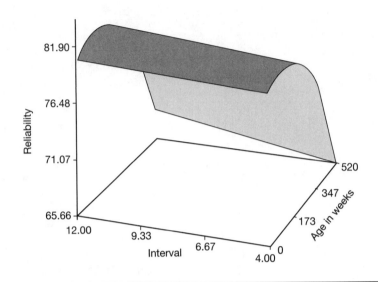

Figure 6.7 Reliability of the fail-safe versus maintenance interval.

A study is designed to examine the effect of start-ups and shutdowns on the behavior of the Kalman filter and database. Artificial data are constructed to simulate the data that might stream from the process during start-up and shutdown. Unless the inspections are somehow timed to production rates, the sampling frequency and spacing are likely to be quite different during these initial and terminal intervals. This unequal spacing has to be handled correctly or it could be a problem for the building of the model used in the Kalman filter approach, as shown in Figure 6.8.

The data from the study show that the efficiency of the system does depend on the spacing of information gathered from the inspections. During start-up the information is fresh, and relatively fine spacing of the samples makes for a model that labels too much of the noise as actual process changes. When the process enters the more stable phase, there is a slight transition as the model retunes itself to run under these conditions. Finally, there is another transition as the normal mode model is still active when the manufacturing process enters its slowdown period. There is not enough time for the model to catch up with the process during this last phase so an inappropriate model is used for a while. Figure 6.9 illustrates this process of overshoot in the model. Figure 6.10 details the actual efficiencies at each phase.

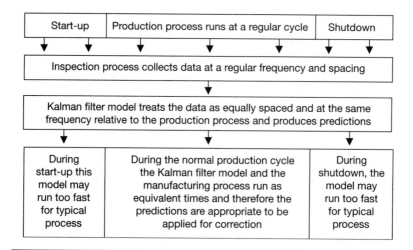

Figure 6.8 Unequal spacing of samples during start-up and shutdown.

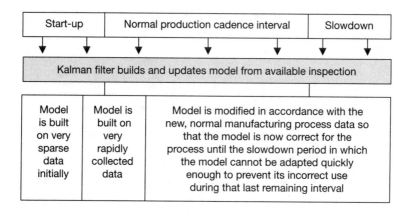

Figure 6.9 The effect of phasing on the Kalman filter mode.

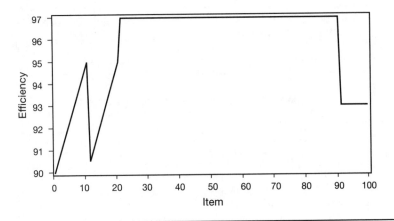

Figure 6.10 The efficiencies during the various production phases.

Chapter 6 Value Propositions

1. Inspection adjustment plans take action on every input.

2. Kalman filter and PID control are two successful adjustments.

3. Inspection adjustment can be used on processes or products.

4. Inspection adjustments are usually rapid in input and action.

5. Inspection adjustments cannot change system structure.

7

Integrating a Set of Similar Inspections

Each of the three broad categories of inspection quality tools that have been described in the previous chapters can have ample power in their own right. For this reason, their use is often fragmented and isolated from one another. Their integration, however, can lead to much more secure systems that also have lesser cost, greater reliability, and better efficiency. This chapter will discuss the issues related to integration. Chapter 8 will undertake the challenge of integration across categories.

THE FASTENER SUPPLIER CASE STUDY

You are a producer of metallic fasteners for paper and cardboard binders. Your customer has you over a barrel. Because of newly available foreign sources that have just opened up, she is demanding that you drastically improve your delivered quality. In fact, she has insisted on a steep penalty clause in the contract for next year. This new clause states that if you cannot cut your delivered nonconforms to less than 10,000 parts per million (PPM), you will be paying out more than you make off each sale. You'd like to just jettison this client, but her business makes up 40% of your sales and chances are good that you will go out of business if you cannot keep her business for at least the couple of years that it would take you to develop some substitute accounts.

You and your quality manager check the historical records and find that production is at about 92% conforming on first pass.

A quick check convinces you that this is equivalent to $(1-.92) \times$ 1,000,000 = 80,000 PPM! And the customer wants 10,000 PPM! You cannot imagine how to accomplish this, especially quickly enough. One of the middle managers, Isabelle, has a masters degree in statistics so you call a meeting with her. Isabelle suggests acceptance sampling as a possible way to achieve this objection quickly, and give the company enough time to make some real process improvements. You decide to give her a chance so you pull her out of the cost accounting department where she has been working and give her the twin assignments of designing a sampling plan and starting up a process improvement program. Silently, you regret not having had the foresight to start this up long ago. Now it may be too late.

Isabelle reviews the sampling plans that have been documented over the last 80 years. On paper she tries out some simple plans to see if they can help the company with its problem. First, she defines a batch as an hour's production, or about 100 cartons of 50 fasteners each, for a total of 5000. The fasteners have to conform to specifications on length, width, and weight. The 10,000 PPM target refers to any of these problems so she realizes that the target PPM for each performance characteristic has to be even tighter. She looks up the sample size required if she wants the plan to achieve an average outgoing quality level of 10,000 PPM, or 1.0% nonconform. The required sample size per batch is 120 per batch. This is feasible, but how much will it cost to implement? Figure 7.1 shows the average outgoing quality curve.

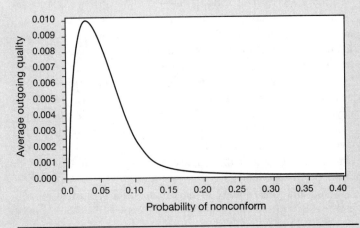

Figure 7.1 The average outgoing quality curve for the fasteners.

She knows that there will always be a minimum 120 clips to test, but she is more worried about the cleansing sample size. Looking at the curve portraying the relationship between incoming nonconform rate and expected sample size, she knows she has to find another way for the expected size at their current production nonconform rate of around 4.5%. Figure 7.2 shows the curve that Isabelle is using.

Isabelle spends some sleepless nights worrying, then has a eureka moment. Looking at the curve showing outgoing quality versus incoming quality with full replacement of nonconforms, she sees that by implementing a sampling process upstream she will decrease the nonconform rates coming to the final inspection. This will cost a lot less.

So Isabelle assigns a task to one of the first process improvement teams created under her fledgling quality improvement program. The team must construct a process diagram showing the points in the process where nonconforms can be generated. She plans to place sampling plans as filters at the critical points, what she calls the quality pressure points, to reduce the flow of nonconforms to final inspection. Figure 7.3 shows the diagram of the process that the team creates.

She fills in the diagram with the details of the rates of nonconform production that the team has assembled for her use. The rates for each product characteristic are given in Table 7.1.

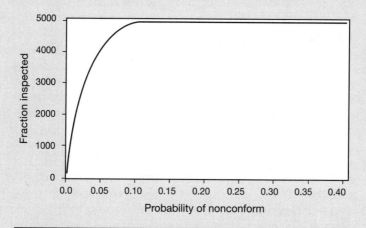

Figure 7.2 Average total inspected for fasteners.

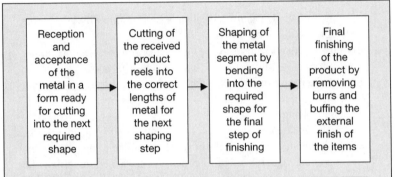

Figure 7.3 The flow of nonconform production.

Table 7.1 The rates of nonconform production by step.

Process step	Length	Width	Height
Reception of metal	Na	Na	1.23%
Cutting operation	1.8%	Na	0.04%
Shaping operation	0.03%	0.12%	0.02%
Finishing operation	0.01%	1.54%	0.06%

She really wishes she had more time because she thinks she can implement some improvement studies using designed experiments that would reduce these rates permanently, but she is under the gun to set something up quickly. Turning again to her attribute sampling plan, she realizes that she can use several targeted plans at the various quality pressure points to create an acceptance sampling system that might give some leverage.

Specifically, she implements a sampling plan at the reception stage for weight, at the finishing stage for width, and at the cutting operation for length. For simplicity she uses the same 110 sample plan at each stage, but now only making the appropriate single inspection. Table 7.2 shows the anticipated average outgoing quality (AOQ) and average total inspected (ATI) for these plans versus the original plan.

This saves roughly 5% in total samples over all three characteristics while meeting the AOQ objectives that were set. Of course, this assumes that the current process stays pretty much the same as it is today and that there are few upsets, but this has not been a great problem in the past few years. There is also a savings

Table 7.2 Comparison of subsampling plans versus overall.

Process step	Length AOQ	Length ATI	Width AOQ	Width ATI	Weight AOQ	Weight ATI
Reception	0	0	0	0	0.31%	3723
Cutting	0.23%	4274	0	0	0.04 %	0
Shaping	0.03%	0	0.12%	0	0.02%	0
Finishing	0.01%	0	0.87%	4187	0.06%	0
Total	0.27%	4274	0.26%	4187	0.43%	3723
Original	0.19%	4462	0.22%	4312	0.26%	4004

in that the inspections are cheaper at early stages because one operator does not have to be trained to do all three inspections. The cost of rectification is smaller in all cases. So the overall savings is even greater than 5% when evaluated in dollars.

THE MEDICAL ELECTRONICS CASE STUDY: AN INTEGRATED SOLUTION FOR PROCESS CONTROL

Consider now the case of a supplier of an electronic subsystem, which is part of the assembly of medical cardiovascular monitoring systems. These systems are extremely reliable if they can make it past their initial burn-in, so currently the process has a 100% burn-in process installed after production, which finds most of the improper subsystems. However, the kit assembly shop, which is the customer for this component, insists that the burn-in process makes their assembly process more difficult and more expensive. They say it is necessary to reduce or remove the burn-in process entirely, and they suggest process control methods as a possible route to achieve this objective. Figure 7.4 shows the current burn-in process.

The current shop manager is an electrical engineer by training and feels more comfortable with applying adjustment systems, but agrees to try the control approach to see if it will work for him. He hires an external quality consultant to come in for a day to train him and his staff. The consultant agrees to make himself available as need be to help with the project.

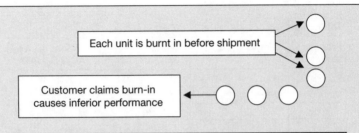

Figure 7.4 The burn-in process diagram for medical electronic devices.

The consultant suggests that they start by listing some of the critical processes that go into the construction of the subsystem as far as the failures. The manager and his team perform a failure modes and effects analysis (FMEA) of the manufacturing process. There turn out to be three types of failure modes that occur with enough regularity to target. Table 7.3 shows the simplified FMEA for these three failure modes with their associated frequencies. All three are severe in that if they occur they would be detected in the burn-in step. So there is no question that the team has to work on them.

The next step is to construct a process map to identify to which steps in the manufacturing process these failure modes might be linked. The team identifies four specific steps in the process; two steps that can cause mode 12.51 and one step each for the other two failure modes, 70 and 72. Table 7.4 shows the link between steps and modes.

The consultant next suggests that the manager perform capability studies on these four steps. They find the results given in Table 7.5.

Upon further investigation, the failures in stability are due to shifts in the process caused by different lots of solder for step 3 and for different crews for step 1. The measurement for step 3 is a force value and so has a skewed distribution, perhaps a Weibull distribution (Nelson 1982). Still ignorant of what this all means, the manager again asks the advice of the consultant. The consultant suggests two types of inspection systems. One inspection is completely new and related to measuring the amount of current that is applied by each operator to the electric equipment used in the soldering process. By installing a read-out with an alarm on every solder, the inspection system prevents the operator from incorrect application

Table 7.3 The FMEA for the burn-in process.

Failure mode	Frequency rank	Severity rank	Overall rank
Code 14.12	5	1	5
Code 12.50	5	5	25
Code 12.51	5	10	50
Code 60	1	1	1
Code 70	10	10	100
Code 72	10	5	50

Table 7.4 The link between process steps and failure modes.

Process step name	Process step number	Failure mode number
Initial solder	1	12.51
Secondary solder	2	12.51
Layout construction	3	70
Packaging	4	72

Table 7.5 Process capabilities of the four process steps.

Step	Mean deviation from target	Std	Stability	Normality
1	.01	5	yes	yes
2	.10	2	no	yes
3	.50	1	yes	no
4	.50	2	yes	yes

of the method. This is inspection applied to the current, which is a process variable, rather than a measurement on the product itself.

A control chart is set up to detect the shift in the solder age. A gage can be installed just after the soldering process to test the brittleness of the soldered joint with a strain gage. In this way, the chart can signal when the solder properties have changed. A Shewhart chart is used to enable detection of the shift as in Figure 7.5.

Further investigation of the unusually high standard deviation for step 1 shows that most of this is due to measurement error. In the short term, before a new and better device can be found, the manager implements a set of 10 repeat measurements on step 1. Since the measurements are independent, this reduces the measurement variance to one-tenth of its original value and brings the overall process variation down to 1.4. With these implementations of control systems, the new capability study shows the following results as in Table 7.6.

Based upon these new processes, the capabilities are as in Table 7.7.

Considering the false positive rate on the burn-in test was about 500 PPM, both the shop manager and his customer agree that this integrated inspection control scheme is better and less disruptive than the current 100% burn-in inspection process.

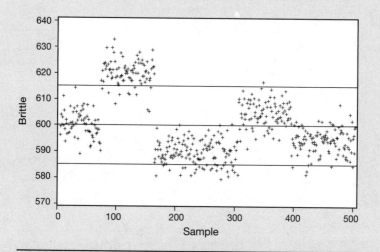

Figure 7.5 The control chart of brittleness.

Table 7.6 Process capabilities after control system implementation.

Step	Mean deviation from target	Std	Stability	Normality
1	.01	1.4	yes	yes
2	.10	1	yes	yes
3	.10	1	yes	no
4	.00	1	yes	yes

Table 7.7 Capabilities of the processes after control application implementation.

Step	Cp	Cpk	Expected out of tolerance
1	3.1	3.0	100 PPM
2	2.8	2.5	150 PPM
3	4.2	4.0	10 PPM
4	3.8	3.8	60 PPM
Total			320 PPM

More generally, the manager can see that he can select targets for each process step that will meet his overall needs. He is good at programming in spreadsheets so he writes some code to simulate the process in which the inputs are distributions for each steps, their parameters, such as mean and standard deviation, and the tolerances. Then he can generate pseudo variates at each step and see what the resulting leak rates will be. He can also add cost to the steps so he works out the least costly way to do this as well. To find the best combination he simply sorts the combinations by total cost after a large number of runs. The results of his simulation confirm that his solution is one of the ten best, so he decides to leave it in place.

THE HELP DESK CASE STUDY: AN INTEGRATED SOLUTION FOR ADJUSTMENT

Pretend that your friend, Peter, is the manager of a technical department responsible for answering technical calls from customers. Peter is venting to you over dinner one evening that the customers are complaining that the answers take too many steps to complete. In the current system, he explains, the level one provider can only answer simple prepared answers and that is almost never sufficient for his group of callers. This first line is responsible for divvying up the calls to the second line of help, but because this is difficult, 80% of time get it wrong! The second line does not have the information to send it to the right person, so they send it back to a special dispatcher who is better able to make the flow decision. This special dispatcher does a great job and usually gets it right on the first time about 90% of the time, 9% the second time, and 1% the third time. So some callers require six calls to get their answers and the typical case still requires four such calls. The customers are rightly complaining. Peter's boss, the manager of the whole service center, is in the middle of wrangling for a promotion and refuses to make any changes or spend any money until word comes through. She is supposed to get an answer at the next annual review, which is still five months away. This process is diagrammed in Figure 7.6.

You are sympathetic and suggest that maybe some kind of inspection quality system could be used that might help the situation immediately without spending a great deal of money. It seems that the whole process could be shortened by improving a few of the steps. Maybe some kind of integrated adjustment scheme could be applied.

You and Peter take a day and look at the process in detail. You find that there is a pattern over the week about what kind of calls are received. For some unknown reason, calls seem to run in streaks of three to four days on the same topic. For example, there might be an initial question about changing the DIP switch settings and, voila, there will be series of such calls. There will certainly be other topics mixed in, but these clustered topics predominate.

So you suggest to Peter that he consider having his technical crew give feedback to the first level operators. They will still miss until a cluster starts, but if they shift to this as their estimate, they

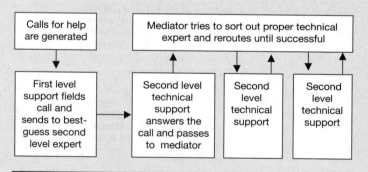

Figure 7.6 Help desk process diagram.

will change their miss rate from 80% to 25%. This is shown in Figure 7.7.

It is also possible to have the expert assigner report back to the first level operators on which calls get sent to her and further update the choices that are made at this level. So the level one operators will have their choices modified in two ways: daily by feedback from the expert users when trends start, and weekly by the expert expediter to help refine which types of calls should go directly to her. Peter tries this for a week and finds that it improves the hit rate at the first level to 75% rather than 20% and finds that even when the first recommendations are off, the expert assigner now hits 95% on the first and 5% on the second, eliminating the third step calls altogether. Figure 7.8 illustrates this modified help desk process.

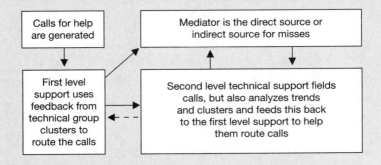

Figure 7.7 First modified help desk process.

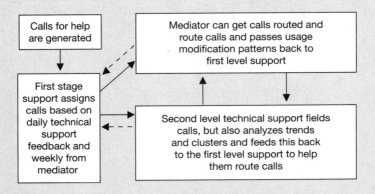

Figure 7.8 The ultimate modified help desk process.

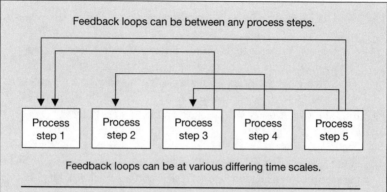

Feedback loops can be between any process steps.

| Process step 1 | Process step 2 | Process step 3 | Process step 4 | Process step 5 |

Feedback loops can be at various differing time scales.

Figure 7.9 Generic system of nested feedback loops.

In general you can see that this integration of several feedback schemes should work well to sort and assign any kind of case. Indeed the approach can probably work on any kind of process where there is a series of events and feedback can occur. The feedback loops can be nested within each other or can be kept completely separate. Figure 7.9 shows this set of nested feedback loops.

Chapter 7 Value Propositions

1. Integration of like inspection systems can be very effective.

2. Acceptance sampling plans can be integrated sequentially.

3. Inspection control plans can be placed throughout the process.

4. Inspection adjustment plans can be tuned to operate in synchronicity.

8

Integrating a Set of Dissimilar Inspections

Building on the examples from Chapter 7, it is now possible to extend these concepts to constructing integrated systems that cross the boundaries of the inspection types. The keys to doing this well are the same as they were in the case of the integration of single types. Those keys are:

1. Examine the process diagram.

2. Locate quality leverage points.

3. Use an appropriate inspection tool at each point.

4. Integrate the performance across the tools.

Clearly, steps 1 and 2 depend intimately on the particular process that is being studied, while steps 3 and 4 are more general and can be abstracted a bit. Remember that the objective of inspection quality systems is to produce an acceptable delivered quality at minimal cost and in a feasible fashion. Although there are overlapping features in all three categories, Table 8.1 tries to summarize the relative advantages and disadvantages of the three systems.

Consider a generic process diagram as in Figure 8.1. While it is possible to treat these entire systems analytically, simulation will be the tool of choice in the book for their examination. This is a flexible, powerful, and fairly robust method of investigation, but there are precautions to ensure its correct use.

Table 8.1 The characteristics of the three inspection approaches.

Acceptance sampling	Control approach	Adjustment approach
Independent of process	Loosely embedded	Tightly embedded
Works on large sets	Works on small sets	Works on individuals
Simple decisions	Intermediate decisions	Difficult decision
Best for slow changes	Best for medium change	Best for rapid change
Robust to distribution	Sensitive to distribution	Sensitive to distribution
Robust to instability	Sensitive to instability	Sensitive to instability
Robust to system upset	Medium to system upset	Sensitive to system upset
Usually for product	Usually process	Usually process

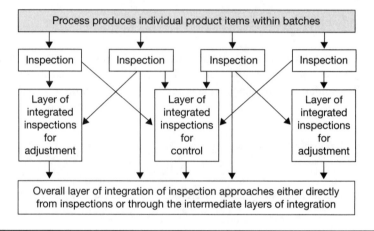

Figure 8.1 A generic model of several inspection approaches.

SIMULATION

Simulation (Hillier 1974) is the use of a model, usually as a set of computer code, to mimic a real process. The model has to be exact enough that conclusions drawn from experiments with it can be applied fruitfully to the real process. On the other hand, the simulation model should be as simple as possible so it can be computed quickly and efficiently. Simulation is so natural to create with computer code that most high level languages like visual basic or C or FORTRAN can be used to build simulation models from scratch. It is usually more economical, however, to use a language that has some specialized features that are tuned for simulation. Use of these features saves a lot of effort and error on the part of the programmer, but, of course, come with additional requirements to manage in order to use them correctly. A minimal set of these features that make simulation easier are:

1. Built-in random number generators from several statistical distributions

2. Easy ways to do loops and track system indicators at each step of the loop

3. Easy ways to control flow logic such as timing lags, and so on

4. Built in statistical functions to analyze the data from the simulation

There are many systems that fulfill these requirements. Simple systems like EXCEL are adequate, but require enormous amounts of work to build up the necessary machinery to do a valid simulation. Slightly better are statistical packages like SAS, but even these are surpassed by dedicated computer packages like FLEXSIM. The three examples that form the basis of this chapter will all use simulation in SAS, but could be accomplished using other packages as well.

THE DO-IT-YOURSELF KIT CASE STUDY

Consider an example in which there is a process to make wooden swing sets kits for do-it-yourselfers to construct themselves. There are six steps to the process: (1) cutting the pieces, (2) drilling holes, (3) sorting and bagging hardware, (4) allocating the correct swings, (5) including the correct instructions, (6) boxing the entire kit. Experience has shown that customers are sensitive to having holes that are incompletely or incorrectly drilled. The company objective is to ensure that less than 1% of delivered kits have some kind of customer complaint. The process is shown in Figure 8.2.

Right now there is no inspection system so there is a blank slate on which to work. There are restrictions on cost, human resources, and support skills that must be taken into account. The drilling process is based on a measurement from the end of each drilled piece, so it is expected that mistakes in cutting will impact drilling mistakes as well. The workers think that these mistakes run in clusters because of setup mistakes. A quick study shows the distributions, their parameters, and the tolerances that are involved in the cutting and drilling operations as in Table 8.2.

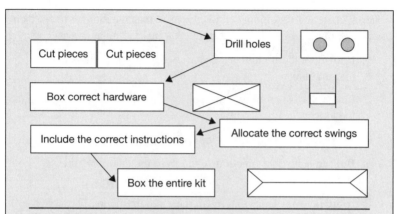

Figure 8.2 Do-it-yourself process diagram.

Table 8.2 Distributions of data for the cutting and drilling operation.

Operation	Distribution name	Mean offset	Standard deviation
Cutting	Normal	20 mm	2 mm
Drilling	Normal	0 mm	1.5 mm

A simulation model of this process would first generate a random variable for the cut length and then a random variable for the drill position using this cut length as its base value. The resulting position of the drill hole is then compared to the tolerances to project nonconforms of sufficient size to cause complaints. In SAS this could be done by generating two random numbers called length and drill distance from end as separate calls to the RAN-NOR function. A third column would be the sum of these two values called actual drill position. A fourth column, which takes the signed difference between this and the target plus tolerance and target minus tolerance, will indicate if they are out or in. A fifth column can be added with an if statement to signal 1 if inside and a 0 if outside. It is reasonable to generate 1000 of these values and sum the resulting errors. Figure 8.3 shows the simulation flow.

Because there are random variables involved in this simulation, it is best to analyze results through statistical analysis. One critical requirement is the necessity to repeat the experiment with different random number seeds. If the seed is not changed, then one will get

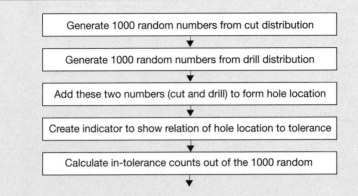

Figure 8.3 Simulation flow for cutting and drilling process.

an exact repeat of the all 1000 results! The simulation is repeated 20 times in this study. First a baseline is run showing the performance of the current, uninspected system. It indicates that the average percentage of out-of-tolerance drill holes is 4.6%. This indicates that there really is a problem with the current system and that improvements need to be made.

Now one can try different proposed improvements by coding them into the simulation and comparing the performances. Note that it is easy to do this kind of comparison, but it is not necessarily easy to find the optimal solution. A single simulation run is equivalent to a single experiment, and one needs to use good search methods and multiple runs (Olafsson 2002) to make sure that the solution is good.

A Solution with a Single Acceptance Sampling Plan

For example, the drilled pieces can be inspected to see if they conform to the requirements. An acceptance sampling plan could do this for a 3% AOQL target. It would require about 10 measurements per batch as a fixed sample on each batch of 100 that is inspected. This is not unreasonable, but it would mean hiring at least one temporary worker for the short term and this is not desirable because of cost-cutting measures that are in place. To simulate this plan we can add a few new variables to the existing SAS simulation code. Namely, we add a new column called batch, which has 1 in the first 100 rows, 2 in the second 100, and so on up to 100 in the last 100 rows. Then add another new column with a uniform random number using the RANUNI function. This will put an arbitrary random number between 0 and 1 into the column. Now sort the data set by batch and the random uniform number. Create a variable marked sample that marks the first 25 values in each sorted batch as a 1, meaning sampled. Mark the remaining 78 with a 0, meaning not sampled. Now multiply the out-of-tolerance column by the sample column. Those items that have been sampled and are out of tolerance will have a 1.

It is time to compute some derived quantities. First find the sum of the multiplied column for each batch. Also find the sum of all the out-of-tolerance values for the unsampled items in each batch. If the sum of the multiplied column is 0, then set the average delivered quality level equals the sum of the out-of-tolerance pieces divided by the uninspected pieces, which is equal to batch-sample size. The average fraction inspected is equal to the sum of the sample sizes for accepted batches and batch size for the rejected batches over the total number of pieces. If the sum is > or = 1, then set aql = 0 anafi = 1.00, meaning that all nonconforms are rectified at the cost of looking at all 100 drill holes in the batch. Figure 8.4 illustrates this modified process flow.

If this is replicated 20 times, again with differing seeds to produce different streams of numbers, then there will be a set of results comparable to the baseline. For example the result might show that application of this approach yields an average of 2.75% nonconforms. Compared to the baseline representing the current process flow without inspection via the acceptance sampling plan, this is a 60% reduction, but does not quite meet the objective. The decision is made to hire the temporary worker in order to implement the plan.

The Addition of an Adjustment Plan

This single inspection plan will work at the cost of one additional temporary employee, but perhaps there is a way to cut this even more. Another option is to have the cutter operator look at each piece after the cut is made and mark it as to deviation from target. This is a quick measurement and will have appreciable measurement error, but it should help. That is, the measurement is made on every piece with a measurement repeatability of 50% of the cutter process variation. This reduces the drill hole variation because an adjustment can be made at the drilling stage. For example, a true cut length that is off 1 mm will be measured to within +/− .5 mm so

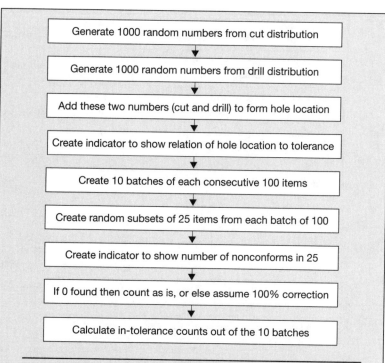

Figure 8.4 The sampling plan adjusted drilling process flow.

that the drill press operator will be able to adjust the process in order to reduce the amount of misfit pieces. The drilling operation will still contribute its full measure of variation on top of this, but the total will be less. Fundamentally this action reduces the cut length from the original $+/- 3$ standard deviations to $+/- 1.5$ standard deviations. This can easily be handled through a modification of the simulation flow as shown in Figure 8.5.

The simulation results from this scenario indicate that this integration of the acceptance sampling plan and the adjustment plan sampling plan is more than adequate, actually achieving a 1.5% outgoing quality level. Since the simulation model is so easy to modify, it is decided to try to find a sweet spot for getting 1% with the least number of inspections. Table 8.3 shows some results, and the conclusion is that the combination plan with the acceptance sampling plan of around 15 samples is best.

Of course this simulation approach opens the way to other possible improvements. For example, the inspections that are utilized in

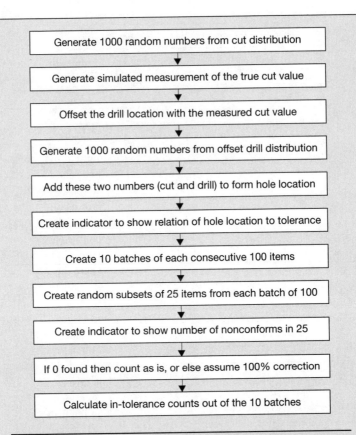

Figure 8.5 The flow of the simulation of the adjusted process.

Table 8.3 Results of several simulation runs.

Sample size	AOQ	AFI	Cost
25	0.87%	56	$87
20	1.04%	48	$76
15	1.23%	31	$47
10	1.44%	28	$46
5	1.74%	16	$27

the adjustment process and the ones underlying the acceptance sampling plan are new and should probably be controlled. Perhaps a control scheme could be placed on the measurements to make sure they are stable. These inspections could be taken every hour or so to determine that the cutting operation inspection process is still stable. The simulation model can be modified to examine these.

THE CHEMISTRY SET CASE STUDY

You are the laboratory manager for chemical testing within a small facility that supplies chemicals for home chemistry sets. Most of the chemicals are repurchased from industrial concerns who have rejected the chemicals for being too impure to use in their processes. They are still usable for the chemistry sets, if they can pass slightly less stringent standards. Your company treats these incoming batches and filters outs common impurities. Your laboratory's role is to take periodic samples and make sure the process is performing to expectations so that the products will meet the requirements for delivery to the toy manufacturer. Your boss has been complaining about the cost of your tests and is questioning the need for the service that your group provides. You speculate that if you provide more of an inspection quality system that directly improves quality, then he may be convinced that your department is a profit center rather than a drain on costs.

The process is simple: each batch is prepared into manageable sizes. They are subjected to a sifting to remove large impurities and a magnetic screening to pick out metallic impurities. They are sorted by weight to separate chemical impurities. The preparation is manual, the sifting is unchecked, the magnetic filtering is done by computer-controlled system, and the weight is performed by an in-line scale. It makes sense to you to try to control with the preparation and sifting, apply adjustment on weight, and use a sampling plan on the magnetic check. The process flow is shown in Figure 8.6.

To simulate this in a statistical language like SAS we can use the QSIM module or write code to generate the simulation model, as is done here. First there is data collection to understand the distributions and their parameters that are associated with each process step. The results of that summary are given in Table 8.4. The preparation process represents the amount of percentage impurity coming from the incoming material or the preparation process. All other steps represent typical decreases from this initial level. Negative impurities are not possible and the target is 1%.

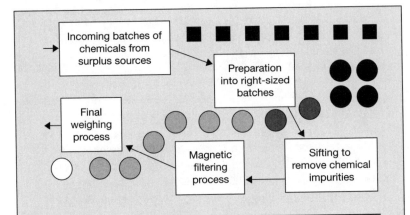

Figure 8.6 Process flow of chemical purification process.

Table 8.4 Data description of the chemical purification process.

Process step	Distribution type	Centering parameter	Dispersion parameter
Preparation	Normal	Mean = 10 points	Stdev = 1
Sifting	Lognormal	Mean = 100	Stdev = 20
Magnetic	Uniform	Center = 3	Width = +/–1
Weighing	Normal	Mean = 2 points	Stdev = 1

In SAS one must create a data set and then write a Do loop to generate the random trials. Because of SAS's excellent random number generators and statistical analysis functions, the effort is reduced drastically compared to simpler programs such as EXCEL. Two of three scenarios will be run to pick a best solution. Figure 8.7 shows the simulation flow.

A first run of this simulation model repeated 25 times can serve as a baseline result. The resulting distribution of impurities by batch is given as Table 8.5.

It is also quite easy to simulate the inspection systems using SAS code. The control system for preparation can be implemented as a measurement control chart on individual values measured after preparation. Because the measurement of the sample for preparation is done with a device with measurement error of $+/-2\%$ impurities and since the equipment cannot effectively reduce any impurity levels greater than 10%, the measurement error limit is set at 12% to ensure that these batches are very likely to be unrecoverable. Any

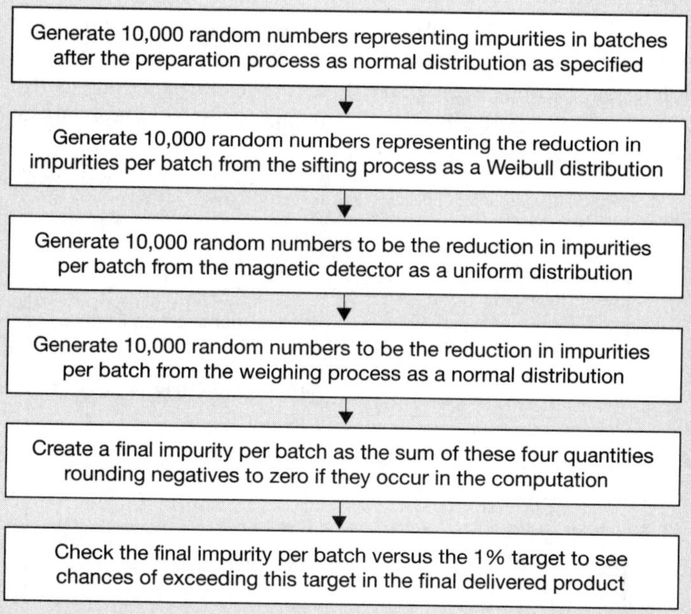

Generate 10,000 random numbers representing impurities in batches after the preparation process as normal distribution as specified

↓

Generate 10,000 random numbers representing the reduction in impurities per batch from the sifting process as a Weibull distribution

↓

Generate 10,000 random numbers to be the reduction in impurities per batch from the magnetic detector as a uniform distribution

↓

Generate 10,000 random numbers to be the reduction in impurities per batch from the weighing process as a normal distribution

↓

Create a final impurity per batch as the sum of these four quantities rounding negatives to zero if they occur in the computation

↓

Check the final impurity per batch versus the 1% target to see chances of exceeding this target in the final delivered product

Figure 8.7 Flow of the simulation of the chemical purification process.

Table 8.5 The baseline distribution of impurities per batch.

Process step	Simulated percent impurities
Preparation	2.18%
Sifting	4.33%
Magnetic	4.85%
Weighing	5.49%
Total	16.88%

batches with measured impurity values greater than 12% are culled from the system since the process cannot hope to cleanse them sufficiently. They are symptoms of a control problem in the purchasing process and are addressed by a separate administrative process. Such a measurement control chart is given in Figure 8.8.

The sifting stage can be inspected by an adjustment system that changes the pressure of the flow according to the measured impurity level from the preparation process. The adjustment plan is adequate to improve the performance of this step from a lognormal mean of 100 to a mean of 70. The results of this improvement are shown in Figure 8.9. Upon running and repeating this simulation 25 times with 1000 batches processed each time, or 10 days, the resulting distribution of remaining impurities is shown in Table 8.6.

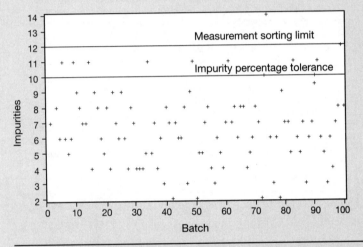

Figure 8.8 The measurement control charts for the preparation process.

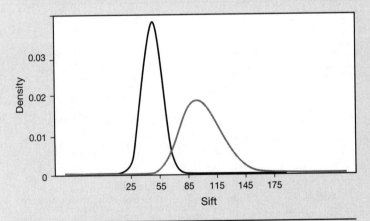

Figure 8.9 The improvement offered by the sifting adjustment inspection.

Table 8.6 The distribution of impurities with integrated inspection plans.

Process step	Simulated percent impurities
Preparation	2.18%
Sifting	0.16%
Magnetic	4.85%
Weighing	2.00%
Total	9.19%

THE CODE WRITING CASE STUDY

Imagine that you work for a software coding firm. Your job is to monitor the production of code for new systems that have already been designed. There are five steps to this process. First, there is a fragmentation into modules by function. Second, there is a matching of the modules to previously validated code. Third, there is a step consisting of whatever small modifications are necessary to adapt the standard code to this new usage. Fourth, there is rough code writing for any unmatched sections. Finally, there is a cleanup of the coding for the unmatched sections. Figure 8.10 shows the structure of this process.

For potential inspection systems, consider the application of quick checks of errors done by checking the logic on 20 lines of code randomly sampled from each set of 1000 lines of code generated at each of the three steps that involve programming. If an error is found in any of these random check sets, then the entire set of 1000 lines must be verified. This system is integrated with an adjustment plan that alters the sample size in each lot in relation to the quality results in the last sample. That is, if the last sample has more than one error, then the next set of code is sampled at double the rate of the first, in other words, 20 lines rather than 10. In addition, there is a control scheme in which the results of the samples from 10 subsets of code are collected. If the number of errors totaled in this set of 10 lines exceeds three, then all sample sizes are raised by 10 immediately and maintained until 10 times 10 lines equals 0, in which case the sample size drops again to 10. Figure 8.11 shows the proposed process flow.

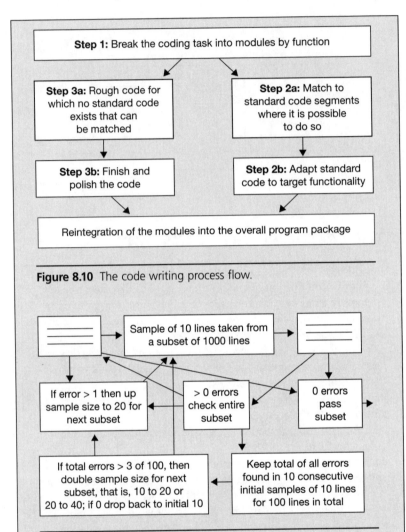

Figure 8.10 The code writing process flow.

Figure 8.11 The flow of the proposed inspection system for coding.

The simulated baseline of 1000 modules replicated 20 times yields an average of 2.4% errors. The inspection-supplemented system simulates an average of 0.3% errors. This is well below the target of 1% allowable errors that was given. The SAS simulation model can be adapted quite easily to handle other scenarios as well. And it has a module to search for a best plan with different sampling rates and rules. It accomplishes this search through various sophisticated hill-climbing routines. A number of runs may be necessary to achieve an approximate best setting of the inspection schemes, but it usually does not take nearly as much effort to find some good solutions.

Chapter 8 Value Propositions

1. Dissimilar inspection systems can be effectively integrated.

2. The potential gain is even greater for dissimilar than similar systems.

3. Acceptance sampling is placed best at process break points.

4. Inspection control is effective for more extreme actions.

5. Inspection adjustment can be effectively embedded into the process.

6. Simulation is a critical tool that can aid in this integration process.

9

Adaptive Inspection Systems

No matter how good the initial design of an inspection quality system may be, it can be made better by allowing it to adapt. Adaptation for an inspection system is the process of changing the parameters of the inspection modules in a dynamic fashion. One might change the sample size in an acceptance sampling plan according to a predetermined fashion in order to break up a potential nonrandom sampling scheme. Or one might change the acceptance number according to observed quality history in a set of batches. In a similar fashion the window used in the feedback loop adjustment scheme can be altered to fit production cycle time changes. Or the weighting scheme in a control inspection can be tuned to provide quicker response to start-up problems, and then changed back again once a stable state has been achieved.

ADAPTATION IN ACCEPTANCE SAMPLING PLANS

Consider the acceptance sampling plan that is one of the primary components of the inspection quality program arsenal. There are at least 10 different broad changes that one could make to these plans in an adaptive scenario. They are:

1. Change type of plan from attribute to variables.

2. Change type of plan from batch to continuous.

3. Change batch size.

4. Change acceptance number.

5. Change sample size.

6. Change clearance interval.

7. Change sampling frequency.

8. Add multiple sampling levels.

9. Switch between type of plans.

10. Do all of the above.

The outgoing quality curve will be used as a measure of the performance of these adaptive acceptance sampling plans compared to the baseline fixed plan. It is often a sufficient way in which to summarize the performance of such plans. Here is a case study outlining an attribute batch plan with only the sample size adaptively changed.

THE TAKE-OUT RESTAURANT CASE STUDY

A fast-food restaurant specializing in Italian food is trying to improve its ability to meet orders. The current process is for a window attendant to take the order and enter it into a computer system that displays it on a screen for the cook attendants to make up from either prepared portions or as a special order. The cook attendant okays the order and routes it to the cash register. The window operator then closes the transaction when he or she delivers the food. The trouble is that the rate of incorrect or incomplete orders is nearly 10% and business is suffering.

A consultant is called in and recommends a simple acceptance sampling plan on each order before it is released. The typical order is eight items: usually three entrees, three drinks, two salads, a number of napkins, a number of straws, and a number of special orders. Each of these items may be customized by four sauces, by large/medium/small drink size, or by eight dressings or amounts. There are exactly 88 possible choices to be made either correctly or incorrectly when all these possibilities are accounted. Figure 9.1 shows the fast-food ordering process.

The proposed inspection plan is to implement a check on the delivery by verifying the correctness of four randomly chosen items from each order. If there are no mistakes in the sample, then it is released as is. If there are one or more mistakes, then the order is rechecked for every item. It has also been decided by management that more mistakes can be tolerated during low volume times because the correction of orders causes less jam-up problems then. Figure 9.2 shows the flow of the inspection plan.

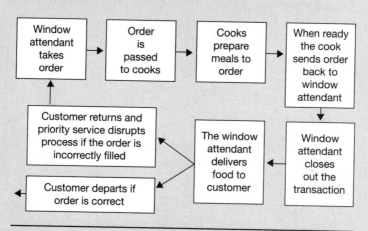

Figure 9.1 The fast-food ordering process flow.

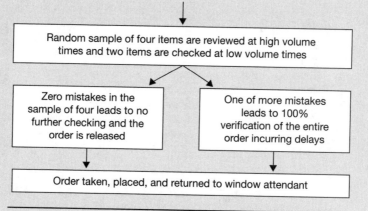

Figure 9.2 Fast-food sampling inspection plan.

Two versions of the sampling plan are chosen as possibilities to be driven by a count of the customers processed in 30-minute intervals. If the number of customers is over 10 per 30 minutes, then the higher sampling rate is used. If lower than 10 per 30 minutes, the lower sampling rate is used. The higher rate requires a sample size of five items to be verified and the lower rate requires just two items. Figures 9.3 and 9.4 show the AQL curve for the high and low rates.

Of course the adaptive aspect of the plan is that it will switch automatically between the two intensities of sampling based on

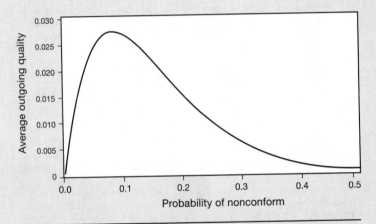

Figure 9.3 AQL curve of high rate sampling plan.

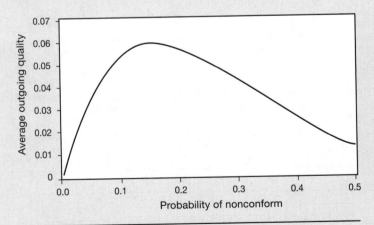

Figure 9.4 AQL curve of low rate sampling plan.

the customer rate during each 30-minute period. A study of this rate over a two-week period shows this distribution of customers per 30 minutes as shown in Figure 9.5.

The actual performance of the plan will depend on the number of switches made and that depends on the observed customer rates, but if the historical pattern continues then one would expect the AOQ to be 6% for 80% of the period and 2.8% for 20% for an average plan AOQ of 5.4%. The AQL curve for the adaptive sampling plan is shown in Figure 9.6.

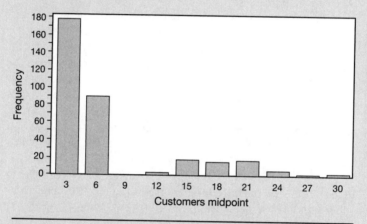

Figure 9.5 Histogram of customers per 30-minute intervals.

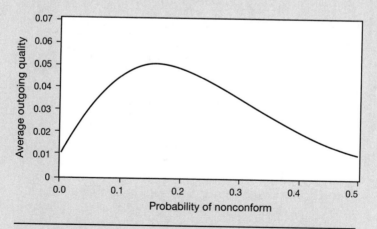

Figure 9.6 The AQL curve for the adaptive sampling plan.

THE TEXTILE GLUING CASE STUDY

The process applies a glue coating to textile cords before their combination with rubber into a tissue. This tissue has to have the right strength to meet manufacturing requirements later in the process. There is a laboratory test for the strength applied destructively to a sample piece of tissue by pulling it apart under conditions of constant force. But this test is destructive and can only be applied sparingly to the process. Figure 9.7 show the process flow of the textile gluing process.

The gluing process is the major determinant of the strength and it can be varied in direct response to discrepancies between the observed and targeted strengths. It is decided to apply an adjustment scheme to the problem of improving outgoing quality in terms of the percentage of tissue that meet the specifications. A preliminary study is done in which 50 consecutive samples are taken from a production run for testing. This is at least 10 times faster than the normal testing protocol allows. The tests are performed and an analysis is made of the characteristic run pattern as temperatures change and the glue pots are emptied. It is found that a combination of a periodic pattern in temperature and a linear trend due to glue pot usage explains 80% of the variation. This pattern is shown in Figures 9.8 and 9.9.

The only difference between runs is found in the slope of the linear trend. If the linear trend is steep, then the control system overreacts and causes the cyclic term to appear. Otherwise, if the

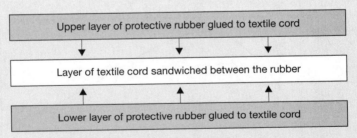

Test of strength of the gluing process is accomplished by taking a sample piece of the tissue and measuring the force at which it separates under laboratory conditions.

Figure 9.7 The textile gluing process flow.

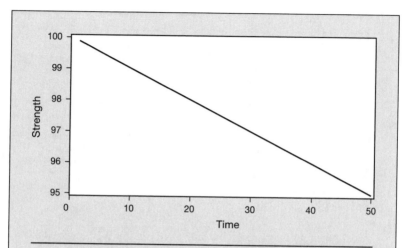

Figure 9.8 The pattern in the gluing strength from glue pot emptying.

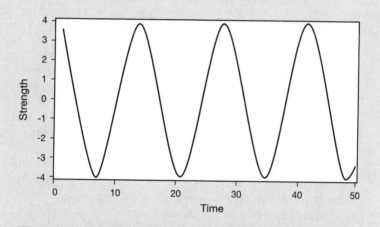

Figure 9.9 Pattern in the gluing strength from temperature cycle.

linear trend is slow, then the control systems compensate well and the harmonic effect is not apparent. So the inspection method is to measure two quick test samples at the start of the run. The slope is estimated, and this determines the adjustment model. If the slope is severe, then the inspection is driven by the cycle. Namely, a sample is taken at the expected extremes of swing. If the trend is

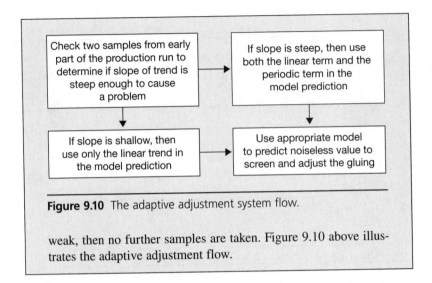

Figure 9.10 The adaptive adjustment system flow.

weak, then no further samples are taken. Figure 9.10 above illustrates the adaptive adjustment flow.

THE PAINT STORE CASE STUDY

The paint store has the task of determining when to order new lots of standard pigments. All specialized colors are mixed upon request by combining the necessary parts of each of the pigments with a white base. Usually this process works fine except that eventually the pigments become adulterated by dirt, dust, and process contaminants, and new ones have to be ordered. Figure 9.11 depicts the situation.

A control inspection scheme is created for the purpose. The plan will have two components. One will require periodic samples to be checked in chromatic analyzer every twentieth gallon. If the sample exceeds a first limit, then a new more frequent sampling is started every fifth gallon and a new batch of standard pigment is placed on order when the result of the more frequent sampling exceeds a second limit. The pigment is pulled when this more frequent sampling exceeds a final, third level. This control inspection plan is shown Figure 9.12.

It is also possible to allow this kind of dynamic adaptation in integrated inspection systems in a clear manner. Simulation can be used to assess different choices and determine the resulting behaviors. It is possible through the use of designed experiments

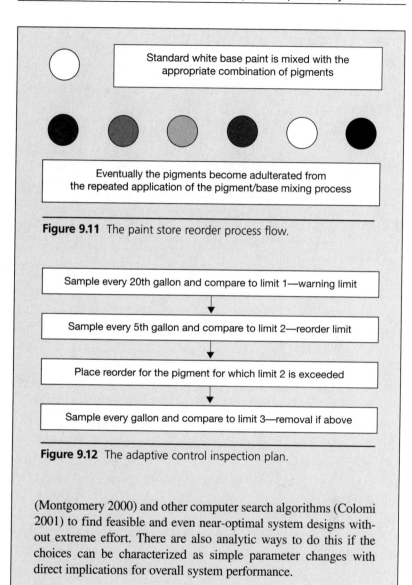

Figure 9.11 The paint store reorder process flow.

Figure 9.12 The adaptive control inspection plan.

(Montgomery 2000) and other computer search algorithms (Colomi 2001) to find feasible and even near-optimal system designs without extreme effort. There are also analytic ways to do this if the choices can be characterized as simple parameter changes with direct implications for overall system performance.

Chapter 9 Value Propositions

1. Inspection plans may be improved by allowing them to adapt.

2. Changes can be made in the parameters of the inspection plans.

3. Changes can be made in the integration of the inspection plans.

4. Adaptation is related to patterns internal or external to the plans themselves.

10

Inspection Systems in Total Quality Management

Two of the more popular and successful quality programs today are lean manufacturing (Womack 1996) and Six Sigma (Hammer 2002). Many companies deal with these programs as separate entities in an overall quality program, and other companies adopt one or the other exclusively. Because of the apparent value of these two methods, it has also become useful to merge the two approaches into one program with a name like Lean Six Sigma. The question that lies at the heart of this chapter is the proper relationship between inspection quality management and these Lean Six Sigma efforts.

AN INTRODUCTION TO LEAN SIX SIGMA

Six Sigma is thought to be a process improvement methodology, but in the true Six Sigma-centered organizations it is really much more than this. Foremost it is a framework of management that is founded on at least the following five principles:

1. Customer focus

2. Strong financial justification

3. Management responsibilities

4. Committed resources

5. Visible organizational infrastructure

Typically the improvement efforts that the Six Sigma program targets are project-based and aimed at reducing variation. Of course, the term *Six Sigma* has also taken on some secondary meanings that are merely part of the overall structure rather than its entirety. For example, *Six Sigma quality* refers to a target nonconform level of 3.4 per million opportunities, which often serves as a criterion for measurement of success and effort. And sometimes the tools that are applied in the process become labeled as Six Sigma tools even though they are often identical with the standard statistical tools of MSA, capability studies, statistical testing, and design of experiments.

Lean manufacturing is an approach that attempts to streamline processes. The lean practitioner conceives of process time as being a combination of value-added time and waste time. By studying the flow through the processes, the relative proportion of value-added time can be raised, ideally until there is no wasted time at all. When this ideal is achieved, there are accompanying simplifications and cost reduction because inventories are low, storage capacity is unnecessary, and personnel can often be reassigned. The tools of lean manufacturing are mainly process flowcharts and measurement of cycle times. Often it is variation in cycle times that cause the biggest losses in lean manufacturing studies.

Lean Six Sigma (George 2002) is an amalgam of the two programs of lean manufacturing and Six Sigma. Primarily this amalgamation means that the methods and systems of the Six Sigma program are applied to the variation in cycle times, flow processes, and inventory management that are critical in lean manufacturing. That is, a project might be initiated to study the wasted time in preparing and packaging materials for shipment. The potential gain would be evaluated according to Lean Six Sigma principles and then this project would be entered into competition with the other Six Sigma projects aimed at variation reduction in product placement, customer service, or any of the other areas. If selected, the lean project would then be funded and management would assign appropriate leadership and support resources to get it accomplished. Tools such as capability studies, measurement studies, and design of experiments would be then be applied to improve the basic times and flows associated with the system. This embedding of lean is shown in Figure 10.1.

Once the Lean Six Sigma project produces a process improvement, its value must be maintained. This is where acceptance sampling, control, and adjustment play important roles. Ordinarily these fundamental methods of inspection quality management are only fully utilized at the end of the Lean Six Sigma project. But they are critical even in this approach for maintaining the improvement and reaping the bulk of the gains.

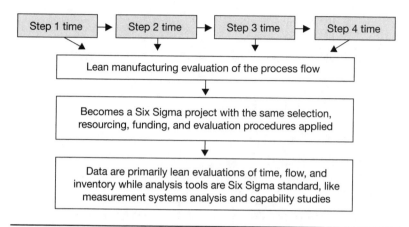

Figure 10.1 A lean project embedded into the Six Sigma program.

Simplistically, the Lean Six Sigma program may be viewed primarily as an organized way to generate good improvement projects and to provide them with adequate resource and leadership to see them through to completion. Of course inspections are necessary to gather data, implement solutions, and monitor gains, but there are additional standard tools such as capability studies, measurement systems studies, and designed experiments. Once an improvement is made, it is critical to design and implement good inspection systems to maintain the gain.

By its very nature, the successful Lean Six Sigma program creates punctual, dramatic improvements in processes. Even in the most vigorous and widespread programs, Lean Six Sigma should not be called continuous improvement of process and product because of this punctuated progression. Perhaps a better name would be continual, rather than continuous, improvement. It is understood in most programs that there will be substantial gaps in time between the improvement cycles. As the success of the Lean Six Sigma programs show, there is nothing wrong or ineffective about this approach. But Lean Six Sigma should be seen as a structure like a metaprogram that surrounds and supports the inspection quality system.

Less Obvious Interactions Between the Systems

In addition to the obvious uses of inspection techniques in the projects that lean and Six Sigma engender, there is another, perhaps potentially stronger, link between the two. This link emphasizes the fact that inspection systems and management can profitably be applied to the improvement of the Lean Six Sigma process itself. To understand the intent of this approach, consider

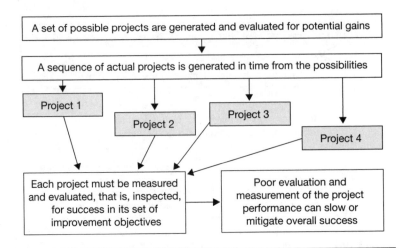

Figure 10.2 The Lean Six Sigma process flow.

the Lean Six Sigma process as a set of projects that can lead to discrete jumps in process performance. This progress is generally measured only at these jump points, or soon afterwards. To find which of the steps is successful, they must be inspected. Typically this inspection is done by the accounting department based on observed and verifiable gains in certain key operating characteristics. The process flow for the Lean Six Sigma is shown in Figure 10.2.

Inspection quality management can be used to monitor and guide this Lean Six Sigma process. Inspections will consist of estimate of success achieved as a match between the project objectives and its deliverables. If the project key operating indicator was product scrap reduction, then inspections could be made at several points, perhaps weeks, and the scrap reduction estimated at each step. Sampling, control, or adjustment techniques could then be applied to these inspections in ways that are similar to many of the examples that have been presented earlier in this work.

THE LEAN SIX SIGMA PROGRAM EVALUATION CASE STUDY

Imagine that you are the director of the company's Lean Six Sigma program. It is one of your responsibilities and challenges to judge the success of each project. It is crucial to do this determination correctly and fairly since successful project leadership is a fundamental requirement for promotion and bonus payment in the company. And, of course, it is crucial to be able to show upper management that your program is working well. There are criteria that have been established for certification as a successful project and these are widely known to the participant project leaders. One critical requirement is that the gain be at least 200% greater than the required project cost. Unfortunately the precise manner of measurement of this gain is not so well defined. The interval of measurement is not specified, nor the sample size, or the method of estimation. All of that has been left to your discretion.

It is clear that you need a baseline measurement and an after-improvement measurement. You decide that it should be possible to inspect the systems and estimate the losses daily for at least six months postproject completion. You divide the total projected gain and make it a percentage of the total costs per day. Since there is no automated system in place to collect these measurements, they will be snapshots of the progress. They are certainly not equivalent to 100% inspection because there are time gaps in which the performance is not measured. At each point of inspection the value of gain will be estimated and examined to see if it exceeds the 200% of the project cost. You decide to track two performance indicators, the average daily savings and the daily indicator of the success, in hitting the +200% target. This project evaluation scheme is shown in Figure 10.3.

You decide that a hybrid inspection system is the best way in which to proceed. The process will be first monitored before project implementation to obtain a baseline. A single daily sample will be collected each Tuesday. This sample will be compared to

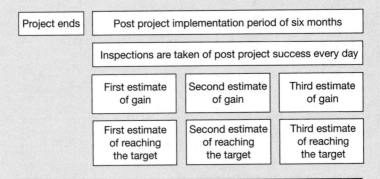

Figure 10.3 The project evaluation scheme.

control limits to determine the stability of the baseline process. If the process point is in control, then a sampling program will begin the next day, Wednesday, and consist of daily samples. If one of the daily samples fails the +200% comparison test, then hourly samples will be taken for the next full day. Otherwise only the single daily samples will be collected. This same approach will be implemented in the six months following the implementation of the improvement to serve as the base of evaluation. The final comparison will ensure that the number of inspections that exceed the +200% target is greater than 90% of the total samples. Figure 10.4 show a diagram of this Lean Six Sigma inspection process.

The approach is evaluated using simulation for typical production data from 10 different processes. First, random variation is simulated in both before and after project phases, and then a graduated set of arbitrary improvements is applied to the postproject phase for several separate simulations. A table is generated showing the probability of detecting a real change in this inspection evaluation system. Table 10.1 shows this probability.

Encouraged by the success of this application of inspection management to the Lean Six Sigma program evaluation phase, you decide to try an application in the project selection phase as well. This is another part of your job responsibilities. First a list of projects is generated by process managers and other shop personnel with an initial cost estimate, benefit estimate, time estimate, and

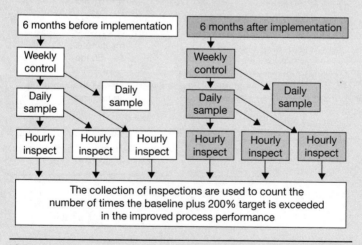

Figure 10.4 Diagram of Lean Six Sigma inspection process.

chance of success. This initial list is reviewed in a session with Lean Six Sigma program evaluators and winnowed to a subset of roughly 10% of the original list. Each of these selected projects is then evaluated more thoroughly for the cost, benefit, time, and chance of success. At this point in this current process the projects are prioritized and scheduled to make use of available resources in a coordinated fashion. Figure 10.5 shows the current project choice process flow.

Unlike the evaluation process, which is brand new, this selection process is well-established and there is adequate history. These data show that only 35% of the projects achieve their stated goals even after the reestimation process is complete. Only 20% of the projects meet their initial rough estimates. The historical data show that the problem of misestimating occurs in all four areas as in Table 10.2.

Table 10.1 The probability of detecting a real difference.

Percentage shift	Probability of detection
0%	0%
5%	50%
10%	80%
15%	95%
20%	99%

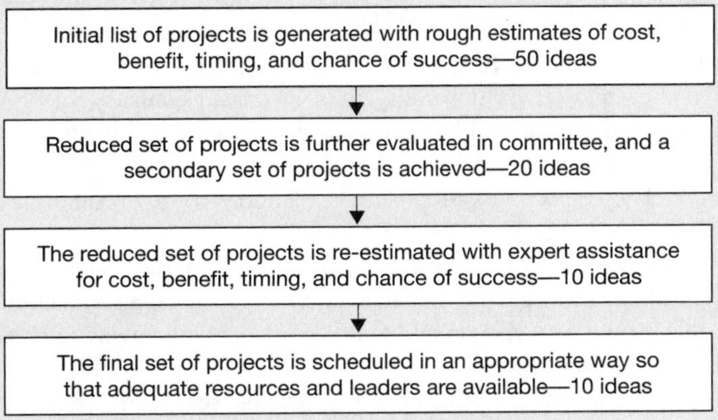

Initial list of projects is generated with rough estimates of cost, benefit, timing, and chance of success—50 ideas
↓
Reduced set of projects is further evaluated in committee, and a secondary set of projects is achieved—20 ideas
↓
The reduced set of projects is re-estimated with expert assistance for cost, benefit, timing, and chance of success—10 ideas
↓
The final set of projects is scheduled in an appropriate way so that adequate resources and leaders are available—10 ideas

Figure 10.5 Current project choice process flow.

Table 10.2 Misestimation problem for project selection.

Estimated quantity	Mean percent over/under	Standard deviation percent
Cost	26%	4%
Benefit	18%	5%
Timing	36%	7%
Success probability	12%	2%

You hope to establish an inspection plan that can overcome some of these problems and bring more credibility to the program as soon as possible. By analyzing the data a little further you discover that there are two important administrative issues that appear to be inducing a pattern in the misestimation. First of all, if the cost of the project is over $100,000, there is a requirement that makes the project leader fill out a written 10-page project evaluation that requires lots of legwork to track down data that are usually not readily available. This longer form does a better job of estimating all the quantities than the short form. This has the effect that the costs of many implementations are underestimated in order to avoid the extra paperwork. There seems to be a consistent downward bias of 10% due to this policy.

Another issue that seems to affect the errors in estimation is due to poor definition of one of the form entries. This item calls for computation of benefit from four sources: scrap reduction, improved productivity, efficiency gains, or personnel reductions. But these items are not defined further in the document itself and require the applicant to search out information in related company files. As long as the accompanying documents are read, the estimates seem to be at least 15% better.

The inspection system should therefore try to accomplish at least two things. First, there should be some way in which to check to see that most people are aware of the documents. Second, there should be some compensation or adjustment depending on the form that is used. But you would like to do this without having to check every project contract.

Accordingly, an integrated inspection scheme is created in order to accomplish these objectives. An extra box is placed on the short form asking whether or not the writer has read the background material that is recommended for complete filing. Of course the applicant may not be completely honest about this, nor may it be correct that they understand the material even if they have read it, but it is worth having. This inspection is made on every application and the evaluation code is altered to automatically adjust for the bias if the box is marked "have not read."

Secondly, an inspection scenario is introduced by measuring the difference between the cost estimate and the $100,000 limit that controls the switching between the forms. The assumption is made that the nearer to $100,000, the more likely the estimates are too low. This is conceived as a curve starting at $90,000 and ending at $100,000 as in Figure 10.6.

Applying this inspection strategy in a pilot program shows a 50% reduction in error in all categories. The summary of this improvement is shown as Table 10.3.

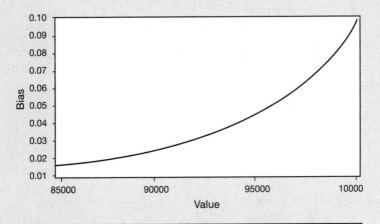

Figure 10.6 The assumed relationship between bias and the limit.

Table 10.3 Improvements shown by inspection policy.

Quantity	Preinspection average	Postinspection average
Cost	26%	10%
Benefit	18%	12%
Timing	36%	30%
Probability of success	12%	6%

In summary, there are many points of intersection between inspection systems and standard process management systems. Luckily, most modern systems still rely on inspection systems heavily and it should not be a major problem to improve them in the ways directed in this book.

Chapter 10 Value Propositions

1. Six Sigma targets solid project gains through dispersion reduction.

2. Lean manufacturing aims to remove process flow difficulties.

3. Inspection is used for studies in both programs.

4. Inspection is often used to maintain the accomplished gains.

5. Inspection can be used to help manage the Lean Six Sigma program itself.

11

Inspecting the Future

A REVIEW OF THE PROGRESS SO FAR

This book has tried to establish a proactive, productive role for inspection-based quality management. Inspections are measurements coupled with intelligence. Both of these components have been improved and strengthened by the extensive developments in electronics and computer technology. Sensors are now available to react to light, heat, temperature, pressure, stress, strain, sound, vibration, chemicals, magnetism, and many more stimulations besides these. The sensors come in smaller, more robust, and cheaper packages and can be interfaced with more systems than ever before. They can even be made intelligent with microprocessors embedded in chips in the sensors. Sensors are now being distributed throughout manufacturing processes and the data they collect are being processed and stored in specially constructed data warehouses. The sensors themselves can be distributed in networks and unusual topologies.

But sensor technology is not the only area in which inspection technology has benefited. The utilization of the sensor outputs has now been improved as well. If human inspectors are used, they are being upgraded in training and environmental conditions. Their natural abilities are being enhanced with devices for magnifying readouts, for removing distractions, and for focusing of the response of immediate interest. And more than ever in the past, human inspectors are being replaced or supplemented by automatic inspection devices. These devices might be as simple as applying a filter to the output to isolate a particular frequency or they may look for a particular profile of frequencies. They might employ artificial intelligences to automatically categorize the results. And they may be embedded in powerful computers performing sophisticated analyzes that no human could accomplish quickly enough. Once the computer is involved it also becomes possible to tie into historical data to judge trends and make intelligent decisions.

Inspections are the drivers for many kinds of actions that are related to continuous improvement of the quality of the delivered product. Inspections can be used to sort products by quality before they are delivered to the customer. Marginal or nonconforming products can be scrapped or corrected to avoid their delivery to the customer. Depending on the type of process and its accessibility, it might be most cost-effective to do this inspection at the beginning, in the middle, or at the end of the production process. As a general rule it is cheaper to catch the problems as early as possible in the process, but details will determine each case uniquely. If the process can be assured to produce no nonconforms, then inspection can be driven to a minimum. This is product control.

Inspections can also be used to drive process modification directly. Often it is a product characteristic like width or strength that is measured and then related back to the process settings that caused it. This feedback can be nearly instantaneous, as in a thermostat, or can have delays purposely embedded in it. Or the actions can be stratified. The simplest fashion is a system with two conditions: take action when the deviation from target is above a threshold, or take no action when the deviation is smaller. Sometimes the actions can be explicitly specified, but this is not required. These inspections can be done on every individual piece of product but more often they are done on a sampling basis. In a very tight feedback the frequency is usually very fast. In a parts industry the inspections are often done on a more widely spaced periodic basis, perhaps every 20 parts or every hour in a shift. Inspections that are difficult or time-consuming are often taken even more widely, perhaps at the start-ups of runs or every day or on an audit basis. These are still inspections and they are still used to control process or product in a continuous improvement approach.

Even process improvement that is done in stages or on project-basis is driven by inspections. Usually these inspections are done on a one-off study basis and then analyzed to drive the next experiment and so on. Highly successful quality programs such as Six Sigma or lean manufacturing depend on inspections in this way.

It is convenient to think about general inspections plans as belonging to one of three major groups. One group is acceptance sampling. Acceptance sampling is characterized by sampling of a set of products on the basis of a particular characteristic. Based on specified acceptance rules, the set of products remains on the current sampling frequency or shifts to a higher rate upon evidence of poorer quality. There are many varieties and variations of acceptance sampling plans that are available, but a fundamental character-istic is the actions involve modification of further inspection. This can be in terms of frequency, intensity, or even type of inspection. Acceptance sampling has historically been applied on finished products by human inspectors, but it can often be more effective when it is applied earlier in the process and supplemented with automatic inspections.

Another fundamental category of inspection approach is the control application. In control, the inspection is taken and compared to a decision threshold. If the threshold is exceeded, an action is taken either directly on the product itself or on the process. Often there can be multiple thresholds and multiple action rules as well. A classic example is the process control chart that is the mainstay of statistical process control. These classic applications typically have two control limits and several actions rules that are left up to the expertise of the inspector or operator. Typically the inspections for a control application are of a moderate frequency that is seldom varied, but more modern applications can be much more dynamic.

The third fundamental approach in which one can classify inspections is adjustment. In this case there is no threshold, but each inspection is acted upon. For practicality, these individual inspections are often filtered and control actions are modulated, but in the simplest approach, each inspection results in direct modification of the process settings. Often the inspections that are used as part of an adjustment approach are done quite rapidly and usually modifications are focused on the process, but it is possible to design adjustment systems for product on an infrequently sampled basis. As the ability to manipulate and analyze in-line inspections has rapidly grown, the methods and models that serve as the foundation for adjustment methods have grown to be quite sophisticated.

Each of these inspections can be adapted and modified separately to be quite effective for continuous improvement of delivered product. But there is even more efficiency and effectiveness to be gained by integrating multiple inspections in an overall system. This can take the form of several acceptance sampling plans staged throughout the process. By tuning the various plans it is possible to dramatically improve the outgoing quality in a cost-effective way. Similarly, multiple control inspections can be tailored in such a way that, as a system, they complement and support each other. Adjustment systems can also be integrated among themselves in this same way to make great gains in quality improvement.

A second type of integration, one that occurs among several types of inspection systems, can be even more powerful. For example, an inspection control process can screen first-stage product that is likely to give marginal results later on. Then in the middle of the process, an adjustment inspection can be used to adjust each product in a more or less continuous fashion.

Finally, an acceptance sampling plan can be used at the shipping dock to catch any special causes or procedural mistakes. The proper selection of the right tools for each process stage and their integration can be quite effectively accomplished through computer simulation or via optimization procedures. The potential for improvement is greatest for this hybrid integration of diverse inspection approaches.

Since inspections are such a fundamental part of product control, process control, and improvement, it is small wonder that they fit neatly within the popular continuous improvement umbrella programs like lean manufacturing and Six Sigma. There are three major ways in which inspection-based systems can strengthen and support these overarching programs: support for analysis, maintenance of performance, and program evaluation. In the case of analysis support, inspections are the manner in which data are collected for the various studies on which improvements are based. The frequency, type, and intensity of the inspections can have a major impact on the success of the projects. One can miss great opportunities because the inspection data are unavailable or difficult to obtain. And one can overestimate impact by collecting the inspections according to faulty or disorganized plans.

When the quality program has formulated an improvement and is ready to implement it, it becomes necessary to consider the maintenance of the imposed modification. Often it is an inspection system that is used to do this. This might be an audit acceptance sampling plan that randomly reviews the work procedure or an automatic in-line inspection administered through a checklist. It might also be a periodic sampling of results that leads to corrective or control actions to bring the process back to its intended performance level.

A third way in which inspections are used in conjunction with quality administrative programs like lean and Six Sigma is not as obvious as the previous two. Inspections can also be made part of the program progress itself. This can be thought of a sort of meta-level analysis of the program. It sits above the action and is used to evaluate and guide the choices of projects, team members, and evaluation methods. In this case the inspections are applied to the projects gains themselves and are often economically based. For example, the rate of profit might be used as an indicator of progress.

THE FUTURE OF INSPECTIONS

It is an economic truth that it is least expensive to perform no inspections at all if the product is of perfect quality once it is handed over to the ultimate end customer. Realistically, most industries, service companies, and businesses are far from achieving this ideal situation. Even in the those companies that have achieved high levels of Six Sigma success, there are still unanticipated nonconforms that can have a significant cost associated with them. Many companies struggle to maintain quality levels in the high 90 percents. Although progress has been made in moving to prevention rather than correction, it is true that even today inspection is the primary way in which high quality is maintained as a consistent level for the customer.

But there have been significant changes in the way this inspection resource is utilized compared to the situation even 20 years ago. Inspections have been pushed back into the process, upstream from the shipping dock. Doing this often results in more inspections rather than less, but the cost of correction can be dramatically smaller when early detection is possible. The initial mistake can be compounded when further process steps add labor, materials, and time to the budget sheet. The inspections have also been designed to be less intrusive to the process, resulting in fewer processing losses. Noncontact systems employing cameras, lasers, and magnetic flux detectors are becoming more and more commonplace. Generally the process does not have to be halted or even slowed to get good inspections through the application of these approaches. Additionally these inspections have often become automated. The devices can be activated, the data collected, the results analyzed, and actions taken automatically through computer-controlled connections.

It is probably impossible to predict the future of sensor and computer development to any accuracy, but it seems clear that there will be some general trends that can be counted on to make inspection systems even more powerful than they already are. Judging by today's trends one should expect inspection systems to become: (1) smaller, (2) faster, (3) cheaper, (4) smarter, (5) more communicative, and (6) more proactive. Each of these will, of course, even more completely enable the methods that are described in this book. But they will also open up new possibilities and problems. It is also clear that with global competition driving quality to better and better levels that all this new potential will not go to waste as smart companies integrate ever more tightly into their quality systems.

Inspection sensors are already small, but expect them to get even smaller. There are limitations depending on the type of sensor that one employs, however. Cameras still have to cover an adequate field of view and lasers do a complete scan of interesting features on the product. In general, however, it should be possible to sample ever smaller areas for stress, strain, temperature, and a host of other features. One of the most limiting factors affecting deployment of inspection devices is the need to host them near or within the process. Machinery and systems should be designed from the outset to host these devices and to be modifiable to contain more if the need should arise. On the extreme end of miniaturization is the field of nanotechnology, which could also eventually pay dividends in the inspection arena.

The devices should also become faster. Many sensors today can easily collect thousands of process readings on flow and viscosity in continuous systems today. Similarly lasers and photonic devices can also scan a single product many times per second. Again there are limitations in some areas. Any device that itself has moving parts will probably not get as fast as those without. And mechanical movements will always be many times slower than electronic ones. Some chemical processes that might be embedded in inspections probably cannot be extensively accelerated either.

As sensors become more commonplace and the market demand grows still further, the relative cost of their manufacture should come down. It will likely not be unusual to have 10 sensors in situations in which there is only one sensor today. Cheaper inspections will also swing the tide of continuous improvement activity to more dependence on inspection. The improvement of a process capability from 1 to 1.3 requires less work, in general, than getting from 1.3 to 1.6. Relatively speaking, it will be more attractive to deploy more inspection capacity whenever possible. Cheaper inspection devices also allow the devices to be disposable. This will enable more inspections to be done in situations in which the environmental conditions would destroy the instruments.

It should also be possible to make sensors more intelligent. They should be able to do some processing on their own and this can dramatically shorten the feedback to the process. Smarter inspection devices will also be more adaptable. Such adaptable devices could lead to situations in which the device takes an initial reading, adjusts its own settings, and then performs the recordable measurement. Smarter devices will probably be more expensive, but their added features could lead to potentially significant gains in the application of inspection technologies.

The potential gains are probably much greater if the communications abilities of the inspections become enhanced. Some sensors already communicate with one another by radio in networks. They can coordinate among themselves using simple rule sets in ways that efficiently and effectively cover a larger area of interest than any single sensor can accommodate by itself. Combining this local control and additional communication with a central computer or perhaps several production line computers could make the entire inspection system operate as a coordinated whole. Perhaps it is easiest to imagine an inspection system that can snoop at almost any point in the production of business process under the direction of central controller.

The last characteristic of inspection systems that should grow in its power and utility is the ability of the inspection device to do correction. Enhancements in this direction will mean that the power of inspection to trigger and direct control actions on process or product will also get better. For example, the sensor might measure temperature and, finding it too low, activate a microwave heater to adjust the product at that point. Or the laser width measurement might lead to machine setup parameters. Or an instrument located at point A in the process might signal to a device at point B, informing it that it needs to add a little more weight to its subproduct to keep the total package weight up to standard. Ideally, the end of these improvements will be the near-universal deployment of small, fast, cheap miniature inspectors that are fully integrated with the central coordinator and with other process steps that involve them as customers or suppliers.

A RISKY PREDICTION

It seems that there are several trends that are coinciding in ways that should make it more reasonable and necessary to depend on inspection for quality improvement. First, quality targets are getting so demanding that a few mistakes can lead to large problems, and such mistakes are easier to detect than prevent. Second, the costs of inspection devices continue to decrease while costs of process improvement modifications will likely increase. Third, the extensive automation of manufacturing and business processes makes it easier and more natural to build data collection devices and real-time inspection plans. Fourth, the ability to integrate inspections as detailed in this book will enable practitioners to put all these enhancements together to milk them for their greatest benefit.

To paraphrase a saying about mathematical models, all predictions are wrong, but some are useful. A reasonable prediction about the future of continuous process improvement is that Six Sigma and other programs will focus more and more on designing, implementing, and maintaining integrated inspection systems. Furthermore, this approach will enable smaller, poorer firms to quickly improve their quality levels and will bring service organizations more fully into the fold. Additionally, these inspections systems will be extended to suppliers and customers so the product may be monitored and corrected throughout its life cycle, from birth to death. Lastly, it is to be expected that these strong inspections systems will become an essential part of processes outside of business as well. The world and we, as part of that world, should reap the benefits of these inspection improvements.

Chapter 11 Value Propositions

1. Progress in inspection technology will strengthen it.

2. Progress in systems science will strengthen inspection methods.

3. Need for better quality guarantees will favor inspections.

4. Inspection methods will enable less expensive quality improvement.

5. Inspection methods will quickly become popular outside of manufacturing.

6. Inspection methods will become available in nonstandard situations.

References

Acheson, D. J. 1974. *Quality Control and Industrial Statistics.* 4th ed. Homewood, IL: Richard D. Irwin Inc.

American Heritage Dictionary. 2nd Coll. ed. 1985. Boston, MA: Houghton-Mifflin Company.

Automobile Industry Action Group. 2002. *Measurement Systems Analysis*, 3rd ed. DaimlerChrysler, Ford Motor, and General Motors.

Barnett, V., and T. Lewis. 1984. *Outliers in Statistical Data.* 2nd ed. New York: John Wiley and Sons, Inc.

Bennis, W. G. 2004. The seven ages of the leader. *Harvard Business Review* (January): 46–53.

Berk, J., and S. Berk. 1993. *Total Quality Management.* New York: Sterling Publishing.

Bisgaard, S., and J. Freiesieben. 2004. Six Sigma and the Bottom Line. *Quality Progress* 37 (9): 57-62.

Box, G. E. P., and G. M. Jenkins. 1976. *Time Series Analysis, Forecasting and Control.* Oakland, CA: Holden-Day.

Box, G. E. P., and J. F. MacGregor. 1974. The analysis of closed loop dynamic stochastic systems. *Technometrics* 16 (3):391–398.

Campanella, J. 1999. *Principles of Quality Costs: Principles, Implementation, and Use.* 3rd ed. Milwaukee, WI: ASQ Quality Press.

Carroll, J. M. 1970. *The Story of the Laser.* new ed. New York: E.P. Dutton and Company.

Cochran, W. G. 1963. *Sampling Techniques.* 2nd ed. New York: John Wiley and Sons, Inc.

Colomi, A., M. Dorigo, F. Maffioli, V. Maniezzo, G. Righini, and M. Trubian. 2001. Heuristics from nature for hard combinatorial optimization problems. *International Transactions in Operational Research* 3 (1):1–21.

Crosby, P. B. 1984. *Quality Without Tears*. New York: McGraw-Hill.

Deming, W. E. 1986. *Out of the Crisis*. Cambridge, MA: MIT CAES.

Downing, D. J., D. H. Pike, and G. W. Morrison. 1980. Application of the Kalman filter to inventory control. *Technometrics* 22 (1):17–22.

English, L. P. 1999. *Improving Data Warehouse and Business Information Quality: Methods for Reducing Costs and Increasing Profits*. New York: John Wiley and Sons.

Fudenberg, D., and K. Levine. 1998. *Learning in Games*. Cambridge, MA: MIT Press.

Garvin, D. A. 1988. *Managing Quality*. New York: The MacMillan Company.

George, M. 2002. *Lean Six Sigma: Combining Six Sigma Quality with Lean Speed*. New York: McGraw-Hill.

Goldratt, E. 1990. *Theory of Constraints*. Great Barrington, MA: North River Press.

Grant, E., and R. S. Leavenworth. 1996. *Statistical Quality Control*. New York: McGraw-Hill.

Hammer, M. 2002. Process management and the future of Six Sigma. *Sloan Management Review*. 43 (2):26–32.

Harmon, P., and D. King. 1985. *Expert Systems*. New York: John Wiley and Sons, Inc.

Henley, E. J., and H. Kumamoto. 1981. *Reliability Engineering and Risk Assessment*. Englewood Cliffs, NJ: Prentice Hall Inc.

Hiller, F. S., and G. J. Lieberman. 1974. *Operations Research*. 2nd ed. San Francisco: Holden-Day.

Huang, G. T. 2003. Casting the wireless sensor net. *Technology Review* July-August, 51–56.

Juran, J. M. 1999. *Juran's Quality Handbook*. 5th ed. New York: McGraw-Hill.

Kennedy, J., R. C. Eberhart, and Y. Shi. 2001. *Swarm Intelligence*. San Francisco: Morgan-Kaufmann.

Lawless, J. F. 1983. Statistical methods in reliability. *Technometrics* 25 (4): 305–316.

Lieberman, G. 1965. Statistical process control and the impact of automatic process control. *Technometrics* 7 (3):283–292.

Liker, J., ed. 1997. *Becoming Lean: Inside Stories of U. S. Manufacturers*. Portland, OR: Productivity Press.

Meeker, W. Q. Reliability: The Other Dimension of Quality. http://www.public.iastate.edu/~wqmeeker/ slide_psnups/youden_address_slides_psnup.pdf

Montgomery, D. C. 2001. *Introduction to Statistical Quality Control*, 4th ed. New York: John Wiley and Sons, Inc.

Montgomery, D. C. 2000. *Design and Analysis of Experiments*. 5th ed. New York: John Wiley and Sons, Inc.

Morrice, D. J., J. Butler, and P. W. Mullarkey. 1998. An approach to ranking and selection for multiple performance measure. *Proceedings of the Winter Simulation Conference*, 719–725. http://www.informs-cs.org/wsc98papers/096.pdf.

Murray-Smith, D. J. 1995. *Continuous System Simulation*. New York: Chapman-Hall.

Nelson, W. 1982. *Applied Life Data Analysis*. New York: John Wiley and Sons, Inc.

Olafsson, S., and J. Kim. 2002. Simulation optimization. In *Proceedings of 2002 Winter Simulation Conference*. 79–64. http:// www.informs-cs.org/wsc02papers/011.pdf.

Ott, L. 1984. *An Introduction to Statistical Methods and Data Analysis* 2nd ed. Boston MA: PWS Publishers.

Pande, P., and T. Gaebler. 1992. *The Six Sigma Way*. New York: McGraw-Hill.

Prigogine, I., and I. Stengers. 1984. *Order Out of Chaos*. New York: Bantam Books.

Rust, R. T., T. Keiningham, S. Clemens, and A. Zahorik. 1999. Return on quality at Chase Manhattan Bank. *Interfaces* 29 (2): 62–72.

Ryan, T. P. 1989. *Statistical Methods for Quality Improvement*. New York: John Wiley and Sons, Inc.

Schilling, E. G. 1982. *Acceptance Sampling in Quality Control*. New York: Marcel Dekker.

Schwartz, M., and L. Shaw. 1975. *Signal Processing*. New York: McGraw-Hill.

Shingo, S., 1987. *The Poke-Yoke System—Zero defects: zero control*. Stamford, CT: Productivity Press.

Stamatis, D. H. 1995. *Failure Mode and Effects Analysis: FMEA from Theory to Execution*. Milwaukee, WI: ASQ Quality Press.

Womack, J., and D. Jones. 1996. *Lean Thinking: Banish Waste and Create Wealth in Your Corporation*. New York: Simon and Schuster.

Index